Reclaim. Piece x Peace

Vol: One - Signature Edition

TAIYE

© 2025 The Tatiana Collection LLC in partnership with TAIYE

ISBN #: 978-1-965210-14-7

Published by The Tatiana Collection LLC

All rights reserved. No part of this journal/publication may be reproduced, stored in a retrieval system, or transmitted in any form or by any means, electronic, mechanical, photocopying, recording, scanning, or otherwise, except as permitted under Section 107 or 108 of the 1976 United States Copyright Act whatsoever without express written permission from the author, except in the case of brief quotations embodied in critical articles and reviews. For any inquiries, please contact the publisher directly.

Limit of Liability/Disclaimer of Warranty: While the publisher and author have used their best efforts in preparing this book/journal, they make no representations or warranties with respect to the accuracy or completeness of the contents of this book/journal and specifically disclaim any implied warranties. The advice and strategies contained herein may not be suitable for your situation; please consult a professional where appropriate. Neither the publisher nor author shall be liable for any loss of profit or any other emotional, physical, spiritual and mental distress and damages, including but not limited to special, incidental, consequential, or other damages.

For general information on our other products and services, please contact our Customer Support within the United States at support@taiye.co.

The Tatiana Collection LLC, in partnership with TAIYE, publishes its books in a variety of electronic formats. Some content that appears in print may not be available in electronic books.

This Journal Belongs To

_____

Dedicated To Those Who Are Ready To Set Their Souls Free.

TABLE OF CONTENTS

Introduction 6
How To Use This Journal 8
About My Relationship 10
Introspection 17
Act One: It Tried To Destroy Me 24
Act Two: Now I'm Back 167
Act Three: I'm Not Just Anybody 250
Reclaim Yourself Affirmation Cards 328

INTRODUCTION

Words are sacred, divine instruments of power—capable of creation, transformation, and even destruction. They are the architects of our reality, shaping the landscapes of our experiences and sculpting the contours of our identity. In the beginning, there was the Word, and through both the spoken and written word, life itself unfolds. Your unique voice is a masterpiece waiting to be revealed.

Reclaim. Piece x Peace is not just a journal; it is an invitation to liberate your soul. Let your words serve as a sanctuary, a sacred haven where raw emotions are given form, and the journey of healing begins. This is far more than a chronicle of heartbreak—it is a testament to your resilience and evolution, a narrative of your strength and rebirth.

Allow this journal to become your confidante, a silent witness to your unfolding story. Honor your emotions, however tumultuous they may be. Let your words become the compass that guides you through life's storms. And remember, even in the darkest of moments, your pen will always illuminate the path ahead, a beacon of hope.

As you fill these pages, you will cultivate an intimate connection with your innermost self. Words are the seeds from which new beginnings emerge. Envision a future rich in love, joy, and fulfillment, and let your words be the blueprint for this unfolding reality. With each entry, you fortify your resolve, empowering yourself to take inspired, purposeful action.

Trust in the magic of your words, for they hold the key to unlocking your highest potential. This journal is a vessel for your transformation—embrace it as a sacred space where your spirit is free to soar.

I have created Reclaim. Piece x Peace with the deepest intention of guiding you toward healing and wholeness. May these pages inspire you to live a life imbued with passion, purpose, and love.

HOW TO USE THIS JOURNAL

Reclaim. Piece x Peace is far more than a journal—it is a sanctuary for the soul, a sacred space where your deepest emotions are invited to unfold without restraint. This intimate companion beckons you to unburden your heart, to let honesty serve as your compass as you traverse the intricate maze of your emotions. Within these pages, you will find a refuge for what has long been unsaid, a place to confront your pain and embark on a profound journey toward healing and wholeness.

Your path to renewal is intentional, carefully mapped over one hundred and eighty days. As you move through its three thoughtfully designed sections, each with a distinct purpose, you will break free from the constraints of old patterns and cultivate new, life-affirming habits. The reflective questions woven throughout are crafted to illuminate your journey, guiding you from the depths of pain toward a future brimming with light and possibility.

To fully immerse yourself in this transformative experience, we encourage the creation of a daily ritual. Begin each morning with a moment of mindful reflection, allowing your thoughts and emotions to flow with freedom and authenticity. As the day draws to a close, return to your journal to process and reflect upon the day's unfolding. At first, these pages may fill quickly as you release what has been long held within, but over time, a shift will occur. You will begin to envision a life abundant with joy, fulfillment, and peace.

Embrace the full spectrum of your emotional experience. Grant yourself the permission to feel everything—from sorrow to elation, from anger to gratitude. As you explore the vast landscape of your inner world with courage, you will uncover a wellspring of strength and resilience that has always been within you. With each passing day, you will draw nearer to reclaiming your peace and stepping into the radiant being you are destined to become.

Trust in the journey. While the process may seem repetitive at first, in time, your reflections will evolve. This journal is your devoted companion on a sacred voyage toward wholeness. Allow yourself to be gently cradled by the healing and renewal that awaits.

ABOUT MY RELATIONSHIP

ABOUT MY RELATIONSHIP

Why Did My Relationship Come To An End?

Who Ended The Relationship?

At What Point Did The Relationship Take An Unexpected Turn?

Who Do I Blame For The Breakup?

ABOUT MY RELATIONSHIP

How Could This Breakup Have Been Avoided, And Would That Have Made Me Happy?

Did My Ex And I Really Try To Work On Our Problems?

Was There Infidelity In My Relationship?

What Did My Ex Say Or Do That I Did Not Understand?

What Were My Complaints About My Ex?

ABOUT MY RELATIONSHIP

Did My Ex Ignore Me?

Did My Ex Respect Me?

Did My Ex Treat Me Kindly?

Did My Ex Show Affection Towards Me?

Did My Ex And I Handle Challenging Discussions Well?

ABOUT MY RELATIONSHIP

Did We Know How To Resolve Conflicts And Move Forward In A Healthy, Constructive Manner?

Did I Genuinely Take My Ex's Promises And Declarations Seriously?

If I Responded 'No,' To The Previous Prompt, Why Not?

Do I Believe That My Ex Took My Promises And Declarations Seriously?

If I Responded 'No,' To The Previous Prompt, Why Not?

ABOUT MY RELATIONSHIP

Do I Believe My Ex Or I Used The Terms 'Fear Of Intimacy' Or 'Fear Of Commitment' As An Excuse For Unwanted Behavior?

Do I Believe That My Ex And I Were Passive About Issues?

Do I Believe That My Ex And I Deliberately Kept Things Light To Avoid Confronting Deeper Issues?

How Would I Characterize My Ex With Both Positive And Negative Descriptors?

Did I Feel That My Ex Was Able To Genuinely Express Himself?

ABOUT MY RELATIONSHIP

Do I Belive That My Ex Was Always Honest With Me?

Did I Have And Show Respect To My Ex?

If I Responded 'No,' To The Previous Prompt, Were There Too Many Wrongs That Needed To Be Made Right Before I Could Truly Respect My Ex?

INTROSPECTION

INTROSPECTION

Did I Feel Like I Was Being Controlled In The Relationship?

Honestly, Did I Obsess Over My Ex's Every Move?

Did I Trust My Ex?

Did I Believe I Was Being Neglected In My Relationship?

If I Responded 'Yes' To The Previous Prompt, Why Did I Believe This?

INTROSPECTION

Did I Feel Rejected In My Relationship?

If I Responded 'Yes' To The Previous Prompt, Why Did I Feel Rejected?

When Did I Feel Disconnected From My Ex? (Answer If Applicable)

Why Did I Feel Disconnected From My Ex? (Answer If Applicable)

When Did I Feel That My Ex Disconnected From Me? (Answer If Applicable)

INTROSPECTION

Why Do I Believe That My Ex Felt Disconnected From Me? (Answer If Applicable)

While In The Relationship, Do I Believe I Stayed True To My Personal Beliefs?

Was My Ex Able To Engage In Discussions About Building A Future Together With Me?

If I Responded 'No' To The Previous Prompt, Why Not?

Was I Able To Engage In Discussions About Building A Future Together With My Ex?

INTROSPECTION

If I Responded 'No' To The Previous Prompt On The Last Page, Why Not?

Do I Believe I Was 'Needy' In The Relationship?

During The Relationship, Did I Need Constant Reassurance?

Did I Feel Like I Was Able To Express Myself In The Relationship?

Was I Able To Be Honest With My Ex?

INTROSPECTION

Did I Sense Any Changes Occurring In My Relationship Before I Started To See Them?

What Red Flags Showed Up In The Relationship?

Did I Ignore The Red Flags?

Did I Ever Address Any Of The Red Flags?

If I Responded 'Yes' To The Previous Prompt, What Were The Results Of What Was Addressed?

INTROSPECTION

If I Responded 'No' To The Fourth Prompt On The Previous Page, Why Did I Not Address Them?

What Hurts Me The Most About The Dissolution Of The Relationship?

Was I Happy In The Relationship?

Did I Truly Believe That The Relationship Would Last Forever?

Was I Able To Be Myself In That Relationship?

ACT ONE:
IT TRIED TO DESTROY ME

ABOUT THIS SECTION

This section serves as your personal sanctuary, a sacred space for the early stages of your healing journey. Each morning, take a few moments to engage in a ritual of self-reflection, allowing your thoughts to flow onto the page without judgment or restraint. Let your words capture the depth of your emotions, offering them freedom and release. Embrace the transformative power of affirmations by selecting a meaningful, positive statement, repeating it as an intentional act of self-love that will subtly shift your perspective. Chronicle the essence of your day—your mood, your aspirations, your gratitude. This journal is your trusted confidante, ever ready to listen, support, and nurture your growth.

As evening settles in, create a serene, calming ritual by engaging with the nightly prompts. These introspective questions gently invite you to reflect on the day's events, helping you unwind and prepare your mind for restful, restorative sleep.

Remember, the goal is progress, not perfection. Each day offers a new opportunity to realign your focus and nurture your well-being. It is a chance for renewal—of mind, body, and spirit. Some days may feel imperfect, and that's okay. Your thoughts are recalibrating, preparing for the positive changes ahead. Any resistance you encounter is simply a reflection of old habits shifting, making space for a new, healthier normal to take root. Your resilience, even in the face of challenge, is a testament to your inner strength.

With consistent dedication and self-compassion, you will emerge from this journey renewed, empowered, and transformed.

ACT ONE: IT TRIED TO DESTROY ME

MORNING THOUGHTS

Date: Mood:

I Woke Up Feeling: Today I Will Intentionally Focus On:

Did I Wake Up Today Feeling Better Than I Did   Today I Want God To Know:
Yesterday?

Today I Am Affirming: I Know I Am Worthy Of:

What Do I Believe I Will Need Help With   Today I Want To Release:
Today?

What Will I Do Today That Will Help Me To   Today I Am Reclaiming:
Feel Happy & Relaxed?

ACT ONE: IT TRIED TO DESTROY ME

NIGHTLY THOUGHTS

How Do I Currently Feel And Why Do I Feel This Way?

Did My Ex Try To Get My Attention In Any Way Today?

If I Responded Yes To The Previous Prompt, Explain How:

Did I Do A Good Job Today Of Protecting My Peace And Space?

What Could I Have Done A Better Job With Today?

Tomorrow I Look Forward To:

Today's Breakup Symptoms:

Today I Learned:

Today I Was Tempted To:

Did I Act On The Thing I Was Tempted To Do? If So, Why Did I Give In To It, And What Were The Results Of My Actions?

What Did I Tell My Ex Today, And If I Didn't Speak To Them, What Would I Want To Tell My Ex?

Tatiana's Personal Note: Please Remember That Pain Does Not Last Forever.

ACT ONE: IT TRIED TO DESTROY ME

MORNING THOUGHTS

Date: Mood:

I Woke Up Feeling: Today I Will Intentionally Focus On:

Did I Wake Up Today Feeling Better Than I Did Yesterday?   Today I Want God To Know:

Today I Am Affirming: I Know I Am Worthy Of:

What Do I Believe I Will Need Help With Today?   Today I Want To Release:

What Will I Do Today That Will Help Me To Feel Happy & Relaxed?   Today I Am Reclaiming:

ACT ONE: IT TRIED TO DESTROY ME

NIGHTLY THOUGHTS

How Do I Currently Feel And Why Do I Feel This Way?

Did My Ex Try To Get My Attention In Any Way Today?

If I Responded Yes To The Previous Prompt, Explain How:

Did I Do A Good Job Today Of Protecting My Peace And Space?

What Could I Have Done A Better Job With Today?

Tomorrow I Look Forward To:

Today's Breakup Symptoms:

Today I Learned:

Today I Was Tempted To:

Did I Act On The Thing I Was Tempted To Do? If So, Why Did I Give In To It, And What Were The Results Of My Actions?

What Did I Tell My Ex Today, And If I Didn't Speak To Them, What Would I Want To Tell My Ex?

Tatiana's Personal Note: Things Fall Apart For You To Receive Better.

ACT ONE: IT TRIED TO DESTROY ME

MORNING THOUGHTS

Date: Mood:

I Woke Up Feeling: Today I Will Intentionally Focus On:

Did I Wake Up Today Feeling Better Than I Did Yesterday?   Today I Want God To Know:

Today I Am Affirming: I Know I Am Worthy Of:

What Do I Believe I Will Need Help With Today?   Today I Want To Release:

What Will I Do Today That Will Help Me To Feel Happy & Relaxed?   Today I Am Reclaiming:

ACT ONE: IT TRIED TO DESTROY ME

NIGHTLY THOUGHTS

How Do I Currently Feel And Why Do I Feel This Way?	Tomorrow I Look Forward To:
	Today's Breakup Symptoms:
Did My Ex Try To Get My Attention In Any Way Today?	
	Today I Learned:
If I Responded Yes To The Previous Prompt, Explain How:	
	Today I Was Tempted To:
Did I Do A Good Job Today Of Protecting My Peace And Space?	Did I Act On The Thing I Was Tempted To Do? If So, Why Did I Give In To It, And What Were The Results Of My Actions?
What Could I Have Done A Better Job With Today?	What Did I Tell My Ex Today, And If I Didn't Speak To Them, What Would I Want To Tell My Ex?

Tatiana's Personal Note: You Are Overqualified To Be Holding On To Someone Underqualified.

IT'S NOT THAT I AM BETTER....
I JUST KNOW BETTER.

WHAT I KNOW NOW: NO MORE STRUGGLING WITH WHAT I SETTLED FOR.

ACT ONE: IT TRIED TO DESTROY ME

MORNING THOUGHTS

Date: Mood:

I Woke Up Feeling: Today I Will Intentionally Focus On:

Did I Wake Up Today Feeling Better Than I Did Yesterday?   Today I Want God To Know:

Today I Am Affirming: I Know I Am Worthy Of:

What Do I Believe I Will Need Help With Today?   Today I Want To Release:

What Will I Do Today That Will Help Me To Feel Happy & Relaxed?   Today I Am Reclaiming:

ACT ONE: IT TRIED TO DESTROY ME

NIGHTLY THOUGHTS

How Do I Currently Feel And Why Do I Feel This Way?

Did My Ex Try To Get My Attention In Any Way Today?

If I Responded Yes To The Previous Prompt, Explain How:

Did I Do A Good Job Today Of Protecting My Peace And Space?

What Could I Have Done A Better Job With Today?

Tomorrow I Look Forward To:

Today's Breakup Symptoms:

Today I Learned:

Today I Was Tempted To:

Did I Act On The Thing I Was Tempted To Do? If So, Why Did I Give In To It, And What Were The Results Of My Actions?

What Did I Tell My Ex Today, And If I Didn't Speak To Them, What Would I Want To Tell My Ex?

Tatiana's Personal Note: Allow The Pain To Elevate You.

ACT ONE: IT TRIED TO DESTROY ME

MORNING THOUGHTS

Date: Mood:

I Woke Up Feeling: Today I Will Intentionally Focus On:

Did I Wake Up Today Feeling Better Than I Did Yesterday?   Today I Want God To Know:

Today I Am Affirming: I Know I Am Worthy Of:

What Do I Believe I Will Need Help With Today?   Today I Want To Release:

What Will I Do Today That Will Help Me To Feel Happy & Relaxed?   Today I Am Reclaiming:

ACT ONE: IT TRIED TO DESTROY ME

NIGHTLY THOUGHTS

How Do I Currently Feel And Why Do I Feel This Way?

Tomorrow I Look Forward To:

Today's Breakup Symptoms:

Did My Ex Try To Get My Attention In Any Way Today?

Today I Learned:

If I Responded Yes To The Previous Prompt, Explain How:

Today I Was Tempted To:

Did I Do A Good Job Today Of Protecting My Peace And Space?

Did I Act On The Thing I Was Tempted To Do? If So, Why Did I Give In To It, And What Were The Results Of My Actions?

What Could I Have Done A Better Job With Today?

What Did I Tell My Ex Today, And If I Didn't Speak To Them, What Would I Want To Tell My Ex?

Tatiana's Personal Note: The Older I Get, The More I Realize, Piece By Piece, That I Won't Settle For Anything That Disturbs My Peace.

ACT ONE: IT TRIED TO DESTROY ME

MORNING THOUGHTS

Date: Mood:

I Woke Up Feeling: Today I Will Intentionally Focus On:

Did I Wake Up Today Feeling Better Than I Did Yesterday?   Today I Want God To Know:

Today I Am Affirming: I Know I Am Worthy Of:

What Do I Believe I Will Need Help With Today?   Today I Want To Release:

What Will I Do Today That Will Help Me To Feel Happy & Relaxed?   Today I Am Reclaiming:

ACT ONE: IT TRIED TO DESTROY ME
NIGHTLY THOUGHTS

How Do I Currently Feel And Why Do I Feel This Way?

Did My Ex Try To Get My Attention In Any Way Today?

If I Responded Yes To The Previous Prompt, Explain How:

Did I Do A Good Job Today Of Protecting My Peace And Space?

What Could I Have Done A Better Job With Today?

Tomorrow I Look Forward To:

Today's Breakup Symptoms:

Today I Learned:

Today I Was Tempted To:

Did I Act On The Thing I Was Tempted To Do? If So, Why Did I Give In To It, And What Were The Results Of My Actions?

What Did I Tell My Ex Today, And If I Didn't Speak To Them, What Would I Want To Tell My Ex?

Tatiana's Personal Note: Sometimes, You Must Let Go To See What Unfolds.

ACT ONE: IT TRIED TO DESTROY ME

MORNING THOUGHTS

Date: Mood:

I Woke Up Feeling: Today I Will Intentionally Focus On:

Did I Wake Up Today Feeling Better Than I Did   Today I Want God To Know:
Yesterday?

Today I Am Affirming: I Know I Am Worthy Of:

What Do I Believe I Will Need Help With   Today I Want To Release:
Today?

What Will I Do Today That Will Help Me To   Today I Am Reclaiming:
Feel Happy & Relaxed?

ACT ONE: IT TRIED TO DESTROY ME
NIGHTLY THOUGHTS

How Do I Currently Feel And Why Do I Feel This Way?

Tomorrow I Look Forward To:

Today's Breakup Symptoms:

Did My Ex Try To Get My Attention In Any Way Today?

Today I Learned:

If I Responded Yes To The Previous Prompt, Explain How:

Today I Was Tempted To:

Did I Do A Good Job Today Of Protecting My Peace And Space?

Did I Act On The Thing I Was Tempted To Do? If So, Why Did I Give In To It, And What Were The Results Of My Actions?

What Could I Have Done A Better Job With Today?

What Did I Tell My Ex Today, And If I Didn't Speak To Them, What Would I Want To Tell My Ex?

Tatiana's Personal Note: You Are Not Created For Everyone, And Only Someone Truly Special Will Understand That.

ACT ONE: IT TRIED TO DESTROY ME

MORNING THOUGHTS

Date: Mood:

I Woke Up Feeling: Today I Will Intentionally Focus On:

Did I Wake Up Today Feeling Better Than I Did Yesterday?   Today I Want God To Know:

Today I Am Affirming: I Know I Am Worthy Of:

What Do I Believe I Will Need Help With Today?   Today I Want To Release:

What Will I Do Today That Will Help Me To Feel Happy & Relaxed?   Today I Am Reclaiming:

ACT ONE: IT TRIED TO DESTROY ME

NIGHTLY THOUGHTS

How Do I Currently Feel And Why Do I Feel This Way?

Did My Ex Try To Get My Attention In Any Way Today?

If I Responded Yes To The Previous Prompt, Explain How:

Did I Do A Good Job Today Of Protecting My Peace And Space?

What Could I Have Done A Better Job With Today?

Tomorrow I Look Forward To:

Today's Breakup Symptoms:

Today I Learned:

Today I Was Tempted To:

Did I Act On The Thing I Was Tempted To Do? If So, Why Did I Give In To It, And What Were The Results Of My Actions?

What Did I Tell My Ex Today, And If I Didn't Speak To Them, What Would I Want To Tell My Ex?

Tatiana's Personal Note: What You Do Not Understand, You Will Soon.

ACT ONE: IT TRIED TO DESTROY ME

MORNING THOUGHTS

Date: Mood:

I Woke Up Feeling: Today I Will Intentionally Focus On:

Did I Wake Up Today Feeling Better Than I Did Yesterday?   Today I Want God To Know:

Today I Am Affirming: I Know I Am Worthy Of:

What Do I Believe I Will Need Help With Today?   Today I Want To Release:

What Will I Do Today That Will Help Me To Feel Happy & Relaxed?   Today I Am Reclaiming:

ACT ONE: IT TRIED TO DESTROY ME

NIGHTLY THOUGHTS

How Do I Currently Feel And Why Do I Feel This Way?

Tomorrow I Look Forward To:

Today's Breakup Symptoms:

Did My Ex Try To Get My Attention In Any Way Today?

Today I Learned:

If I Responded Yes To The Previous Prompt, Explain How:

Today I Was Tempted To:

Did I Do A Good Job Today Of Protecting My Peace And Space?

Did I Act On The Thing I Was Tempted To Do? If So, Why Did I Give In To It, And What Were The Results Of My Actions?

What Could I Have Done A Better Job With Today?

What Did I Tell My Ex Today, And If I Didn't Speak To Them, What Would I Want To Tell My Ex?

Tatiana's Personal Note: Love Is Not Confusing.

45

I AM THE BLESSING
THAT I SEEK.

I WOULD RATHER BE
HONEST WITH MYSELF
THAN LOSE MYSELF
IN WHAT WAS NEVER
MEANT FOR ME.
- BECAUSE

ACT ONE: IT TRIED TO DESTROY ME

MORNING THOUGHTS

Date: Mood:

I Woke Up Feeling: Today I Will Intentionally Focus On:

Did I Wake Up Today Feeling Better Than I Did Yesterday?   Today I Want God To Know:

Today I Am Affirming: I Know I Am Worthy Of:

What Do I Believe I Will Need Help With Today?   Today I Want To Release:

What Will I Do Today That Will Help Me To Feel Happy & Relaxed?   Today I Am Reclaiming:

ACT ONE: IT TRIED TO DESTROY ME

NIGHTLY THOUGHTS

How Do I Currently Feel And Why Do I Feel This Way?	Tomorrow I Look Forward To:
Did My Ex Try To Get My Attention In Any Way Today?	Today's Breakup Symptoms:
	Today I Learned:
If I Responded Yes To The Previous Prompt, Explain How:	
	Today I Was Tempted To:
Did I Do A Good Job Today Of Protecting My Peace And Space?	Did I Act On The Thing I Was Tempted To Do? If So, Why Did I Give In To It, And What Were The Results Of My Actions?
What Could I Have Done A Better Job With Today?	What Did I Tell My Ex Today, And If I Didn't Speak To Them, What Would I Want To Tell My Ex?

Tatiana's Personal Note: I'll Work For It. I'll Pray For It. But I Won't Force It To Work.

ACT ONE: IT TRIED TO DESTROY ME

MORNING THOUGHTS

Date: Mood:

I Woke Up Feeling: Today I Will Intentionally Focus On:

Did I Wake Up Today Feeling Better Than I Did Yesterday?   Today I Want God To Know:

Today I Am Affirming: I Know I Am Worthy Of:

What Do I Believe I Will Need Help With Today?   Today I Want To Release:

What Will I Do Today That Will Help Me To Feel Happy & Relaxed?   Today I Am Reclaiming:

ACT ONE: IT TRIED TO DESTROY ME

NIGHTLY THOUGHTS

How Do I Currently Feel And Why Do I Feel This Way?	Tomorrow I Look Forward To:
Did My Ex Try To Get My Attention In Any Way Today?	Today's Breakup Symptoms:
	Today I Learned:
If I Responded Yes To The Previous Prompt, Explain How:	
	Today I Was Tempted To:
Did I Do A Good Job Today Of Protecting My Peace And Space?	Did I Act On The Thing I Was Tempted To Do? If So, Why Did I Give In To It, And What Were The Results Of My Actions?
What Could I Have Done A Better Job With Today?	What Did I Tell My Ex Today, And If I Didn't Speak To Them, What Would I Want To Tell My Ex?

Tatiana's Personal Note: Stop Getting Offended By Someone Else's Way Of Life.

ACT ONE: IT TRIED TO DESTROY ME

MORNING THOUGHTS

Date: Mood:

I Woke Up Feeling: Today I Will Intentionally Focus On:

Did I Wake Up Today Feeling Better Than I Did   Today I Want God To Know:
Yesterday?

Today I Am Affirming: I Know I Am Worthy Of:

What Do I Believe I Will Need Help With   Today I Want To Release:
Today?

What Will I Do Today That Will Help Me To   Today I Am Reclaiming:
Feel Happy & Relaxed?

ACT ONE: IT TRIED TO DESTROY ME

NIGHTLY THOUGHTS

How Do I Currently Feel And Why Do I Feel This Way?	Tomorrow I Look Forward To:
Did My Ex Try To Get My Attention In Any Way Today?	Today's Breakup Symptoms:
	Today I Learned:
If I Responded Yes To The Previous Prompt, Explain How:	
	Today I Was Tempted To:
Did I Do A Good Job Today Of Protecting My Peace And Space?	Did I Act On The Thing I Was Tempted To Do? If So, Why Did I Give In To It, And What Were The Results Of My Actions?
What Could I Have Done A Better Job With Today?	What Did I Tell My Ex Today, And If I Didn't Speak To Them, What Would I Want To Tell My Ex?

Tatiana's Personal Note: Your Happiness Should Not Be Up For Negotiation.

ACT ONE: IT TRIED TO DESTROY ME

MORNING THOUGHTS

Date: Mood:

I Woke Up Feeling: Today I Will Intentionally Focus On:

Did I Wake Up Today Feeling Better Than I Did Yesterday?   Today I Want God To Know:

Today I Am Affirming: I Know I Am Worthy Of:

What Do I Believe I Will Need Help With Today? Today I Want To Release:

What Will I Do Today That Will Help Me To Feel Happy & Relaxed?   Today I Am Reclaiming:

ACT ONE: IT TRIED TO DESTROY ME

NIGHTLY THOUGHTS

How Do I Currently Feel And Why Do I Feel This Way?	Tomorrow I Look Forward To:
	Today's Breakup Symptoms:
Did My Ex Try To Get My Attention In Any Way Today?	
	Today I Learned:
If I Responded Yes To The Previous Prompt, Explain How:	
	Today I Was Tempted To:
Did I Do A Good Job Today Of Protecting My Peace And Space?	Did I Act On The Thing I Was Tempted To Do? If So, Why Did I Give In To It, And What Were The Results Of My Actions?
What Could I Have Done A Better Job With Today?	What Did I Tell My Ex Today, And If I Didn't Speak To Them, What Would I Want To Tell My Ex?

Tatiana's Personal Note: Standards Only Scare Off Those Not Meant For You.

ACT ONE: IT TRIED TO DESTROY ME

MORNING THOUGHTS

Date:

Mood:

I Woke Up Feeling:

Today I Will Intentionally Focus On:

Did I Wake Up Today Feeling Better Than I Did Yesterday?

Today I Want God To Know:

Today I Am Affirming:

I Know I Am Worthy Of:

What Do I Believe I Will Need Help With Today?

Today I Want To Release:

What Will I Do Today That Will Help Me To Feel Happy & Relaxed?

Today I Am Reclaiming:

ACT ONE: IT TRIED TO DESTROY ME

NIGHTLY THOUGHTS

How Do I Currently Feel And Why Do I Feel This Way?

Did My Ex Try To Get My Attention In Any Way Today?

If I Responded Yes To The Previous Prompt, Explain How:

Did I Do A Good Job Today Of Protecting My Peace And Space?

What Could I Have Done A Better Job With Today?

Tomorrow I Look Forward To:

Today's Breakup Symptoms:

Today I Learned:

Today I Was Tempted To:

Did I Act On The Thing I Was Tempted To Do? If So, Why Did I Give In To It, And What Were The Results Of My Actions?

What Did I Tell My Ex Today, And If I Didn't Speak To Them, What Would I Want To Tell My Ex?

Tatiana's Personal Note: You Cannot Change Others, Nor Should You Want To.

ACT ONE: IT TRIED TO DESTROY ME

MORNING THOUGHTS

Date: Mood:

I Woke Up Feeling: Today I Will Intentionally Focus On:

Did I Wake Up Today Feeling Better Than I Did   Today I Want God To Know:
Yesterday?

Today I Am Affirming: I Know I Am Worthy Of:

What Do I Believe I Will Need Help With   Today I Want To Release:
Today?

What Will I Do Today That Will Help Me To   Today I Am Reclaiming:
Feel Happy & Relaxed?

ACT ONE: IT TRIED TO DESTROY ME

NIGHTLY THOUGHTS

How Do I Currently Feel And Why Do I Feel This Way?	Tomorrow I Look Forward To:
	Today's Breakup Symptoms:
Did My Ex Try To Get My Attention In Any Way Today?	
	Today I Learned:
If I Responded Yes To The Previous Prompt, Explain How:	
	Today I Was Tempted To:
Did I Do A Good Job Today Of Protecting My Peace And Space?	Did I Act On The Thing I Was Tempted To Do? If So, Why Did I Give In To It, And What Were The Results Of My Actions?
What Could I Have Done A Better Job With Today?	What Did I Tell My Ex Today, And If I Didn't Speak To Them, What Would I Want To Tell My Ex?

Tatiana's Personal Note: Be Aware Of Your Value.

ACT ONE: IT TRIED TO DESTROY ME

MORNING THOUGHTS

Date: Mood:

I Woke Up Feeling: Today I Will Intentionally Focus On:

Did I Wake Up Today Feeling Better Than I Did Yesterday?   Today I Want God To Know:

Today I Am Affirming: I Know I Am Worthy Of:

What Do I Believe I Will Need Help With Today?   Today I Want To Release:

What Will I Do Today That Will Help Me To Feel Happy & Relaxed? Today I Am Reclaiming:

ACT ONE: IT TRIED TO DESTROY ME

NIGHTLY THOUGHTS

How Do I Currently Feel And Why Do I Feel This Way?

Did My Ex Try To Get My Attention In Any Way Today?

If I Responded Yes To The Previous Prompt, Explain How:

Did I Do A Good Job Today Of Protecting My Peace And Space?

What Could I Have Done A Better Job With Today?

Tomorrow I Look Forward To:

Today's Breakup Symptoms:

Today I Learned:

Today I Was Tempted To:

Did I Act On The Thing I Was Tempted To Do? If So, Why Did I Give In To It, And What Were The Results Of My Actions?

What Did I Tell My Ex Today, And If I Didn't Speak To Them, What Would I Want To Tell My Ex?

Tatiana's Personal Note: Learn To Accept What Is. Accept Where You Are.

THIS TIME IS FOR ME.

THERE IS NOTHING WRONG WITH VULNERABILITY.

ACT ONE: IT TRIED TO DESTROY ME

MORNING THOUGHTS

Date:

Mood:

I Woke Up Feeling:

Today I Will Intentionally Focus On:

Did I Wake Up Today Feeling Better Than I Did Yesterday?

Today I Want God To Know:

Today I Am Affirming:

I Know I Am Worthy Of:

What Do I Believe I Will Need Help With Today?

Today I Want To Release:

What Will I Do Today That Will Help Me To Feel Happy & Relaxed?

Today I Am Reclaiming:

ACT ONE: IT TRIED TO DESTROY ME

NIGHTLY THOUGHTS

How Do I Currently Feel And Why Do I Feel This Way?	Tomorrow I Look Forward To:
Did My Ex Try To Get My Attention In Any Way Today?	Today's Breakup Symptoms:
	Today I Learned:
If I Responded Yes To The Previous Prompt, Explain How:	
	Today I Was Tempted To:
Did I Do A Good Job Today Of Protecting My Peace And Space?	Did I Act On The Thing I Was Tempted To Do? If So, Why Did I Give In To It, And What Were The Results Of My Actions?
What Could I Have Done A Better Job With Today?	What Did I Tell My Ex Today, And If I Didn't Speak To Them, What Would I Want To Tell My Ex?

Tatiana's Personal Note: Love Does Not Create Excuses.

BE SOMEONE YOU LOVE, FIRST.

GOD IS MY BEST FRIEND.

ACT ONE: IT TRIED TO DESTROY ME

MORNING THOUGHTS

Date: Mood:

I Woke Up Feeling: Today I Will Intentionally Focus On:

Did I Wake Up Today Feeling Better Than I Did Yesterday?   Today I Want God To Know:

Today I Am Affirming: I Know I Am Worthy Of:

What Do I Believe I Will Need Help With Today?   Today I Want To Release:

What Will I Do Today That Will Help Me To Feel Happy & Relaxed? Today I Am Reclaiming:

ACT ONE: IT TRIED TO DESTROY ME
NIGHTLY THOUGHTS

How Do I Currently Feel And Why Do I Feel This Way?

Did My Ex Try To Get My Attention In Any Way Today?

If I Responded Yes To The Previous Prompt, Explain How:

Did I Do A Good Job Today Of Protecting My Peace And Space?

What Could I Have Done A Better Job With Today?

Tomorrow I Look Forward To:

Today's Breakup Symptoms:

Today I Learned:

Today I Was Tempted To:

Did I Act On The Thing I Was Tempted To Do? If So, Why Did I Give In To It, And What Were The Results Of My Actions?

What Did I Tell My Ex Today, And If I Didn't Speak To Them, What Would I Want To Tell My Ex?

Tatiana's Personal Note: You Will Never Catch What Keeps Running Away, So Stop Chasing.

ACT ONE: IT TRIED TO DESTROY ME

MORNING THOUGHTS

Date: Mood:

I Woke Up Feeling: Today I Will Intentionally Focus On:

Did I Wake Up Today Feeling Better Than I Did Yesterday? | Today I Want God To Know:

Today I Am Affirming: I Know I Am Worthy Of:

What Do I Believe I Will Need Help With Today?   Today I Want To Release:

What Will I Do Today That Will Help Me To Feel Happy & Relaxed? | Today I Am Reclaiming:

ACT ONE: IT TRIED TO DESTROY ME

NIGHTLY THOUGHTS

How Do I Currently Feel And Why Do I Feel This Way?

Did My Ex Try To Get My Attention In Any Way Today?

If I Responded Yes To The Previous Prompt, Explain How:

Did I Do A Good Job Today Of Protecting My Peace And Space?

What Could I Have Done A Better Job With Today?

Tomorrow I Look Forward To:

Today's Breakup Symptoms:

Today I Learned:

Today I Was Tempted To:

Did I Act On The Thing I Was Tempted To Do? If So, Why Did I Give In To It, And What Were The Results Of My Actions?

What Did I Tell My Ex Today, And If I Didn't Speak To Them, What Would I Want To Tell My Ex?

Tatiana's Personal Note: Your Biggest Blessing May Come From Your Biggest Disappointment.

ACT ONE: IT TRIED TO DESTROY ME

MORNING THOUGHTS

Date: Mood:

I Woke Up Feeling: Today I Will Intentionally Focus On:

Did I Wake Up Today Feeling Better Than I Did   Today I Want God To Know:
Yesterday?

Today I Am Affirming: I Know I Am Worthy Of:

What Do I Believe I Will Need Help With   Today I Want To Release:
Today?

What Will I Do Today That Will Help Me To   Today I Am Reclaiming:
Feel Happy & Relaxed?

ACT ONE: IT TRIED TO DESTROY ME

NIGHTLY THOUGHTS

How Do I Currently Feel And Why Do I Feel This Way?

Did My Ex Try To Get My Attention In Any Way Today?

If I Responded Yes To The Previous Prompt, Explain How:

Did I Do A Good Job Today Of Protecting My Peace And Space?

What Could I Have Done A Better Job With Today?

Tomorrow I Look Forward To:

Today's Breakup Symptoms:

Today I Learned:

Today I Was Tempted To:

Did I Act On The Thing I Was Tempted To Do? If So, Why Did I Give In To It, And What Were The Results Of My Actions?

What Did I Tell My Ex Today, And If I Didn't Speak To Them, What Would I Want To Tell My Ex?

Tatiana's Personal Note: Accept The Apology You May Never Get.

ACT ONE: IT TRIED TO DESTROY ME

MORNING THOUGHTS

Date: Mood:

I Woke Up Feeling: Today I Will Intentionally Focus On:

Did I Wake Up Today Feeling Better Than I Did Yesterday?   Today I Want God To Know:

Today I Am Affirming: I Know I Am Worthy Of:

What Do I Believe I Will Need Help With Today?   Today I Want To Release:

What Will I Do Today That Will Help Me To Feel Happy & Relaxed?   Today I Am Reclaiming:

ACT ONE: IT TRIED TO DESTROY ME

NIGHTLY THOUGHTS

How Do I Currently Feel And Why Do I Feel This Way?

Did My Ex Try To Get My Attention In Any Way Today?

If I Responded Yes To The Previous Prompt, Explain How:

Did I Do A Good Job Today Of Protecting My Peace And Space?

What Could I Have Done A Better Job With Today?

Tomorrow I Look Forward To:

Today's Breakup Symptoms:

Today I Learned:

Today I Was Tempted To:

Did I Act On The Thing I Was Tempted To Do? If So, Why Did I Give In To It, And What Were The Results Of My Actions?

What Did I Tell My Ex Today, And If I Didn't Speak To Them, What Would I Want To Tell My Ex?

Tatiana's Personal Note: Anything That Is True Will Commit.

ACT ONE: IT TRIED TO DESTROY ME

MORNING THOUGHTS

Date: Mood:

I Woke Up Feeling: Today I Will Intentionally Focus On:

Did I Wake Up Today Feeling Better Than I Did Yesterday?   Today I Want God To Know:

Today I Am Affirming: I Know I Am Worthy Of:

What Do I Believe I Will Need Help With Today?   Today I Want To Release:

What Will I Do Today That Will Help Me To Feel Happy & Relaxed?   Today I Am Reclaiming:

ACT ONE: IT TRIED TO DESTROY ME

NIGHTLY THOUGHTS

How Do I Currently Feel And Why Do I Feel This Way?	Tomorrow I Look Forward To:
Did My Ex Try To Get My Attention In Any Way Today?	Today's Breakup Symptoms:
	Today I Learned:
If I Responded Yes To The Previous Prompt, Explain How:	
	Today I Was Tempted To:
Did I Do A Good Job Today Of Protecting My Peace And Space?	Did I Act On The Thing I Was Tempted To Do? If So, Why Did I Give In To It, And What Were The Results Of My Actions?
What Could I Have Done A Better Job With Today?	What Did I Tell My Ex Today, And If I Didn't Speak To Them, What Would I Want To Tell My Ex?

Tatiana's Personal Note: Life Can Change In A Minute.

ACT ONE: IT TRIED TO DESTROY ME

MORNING THOUGHTS

Date: Mood:

I Woke Up Feeling: Today I Will Intentionally Focus On:

Did I Wake Up Today Feeling Better Than I Did Yesterday?   Today I Want God To Know:

Today I Am Affirming: I Know I Am Worthy Of:

What Do I Believe I Will Need Help With Today?   Today I Want To Release:

What Will I Do Today That Will Help Me To Feel Happy & Relaxed? Today I Am Reclaiming:

ACT ONE: IT TRIED TO DESTROY ME

NIGHTLY THOUGHTS

How Do I Currently Feel And Why Do I Feel This Way?

Did My Ex Try To Get My Attention In Any Way Today?

If I Responded Yes To The Previous Prompt, Explain How:

Did I Do A Good Job Today Of Protecting My Peace And Space?

What Could I Have Done A Better Job With Today?

Tomorrow I Look Forward To:

Today's Breakup Symptoms:

Today I Learned:

Today I Was Tempted To:

Did I Act On The Thing I Was Tempted To Do? If So, Why Did I Give In To It, And What Were The Results Of My Actions?

What Did I Tell My Ex Today, And If I Didn't Speak To Them, What Would I Want To Tell My Ex?

Tatiana's Personal Note: Your Future Is In God's Hands.

ACT ONE: IT TRIED TO DESTROY ME

MORNING THOUGHTS

Date: Mood:

I Woke Up Feeling: Today I Will Intentionally Focus On:

Did I Wake Up Today Feeling Better Than I Did Yesterday?   Today I Want God To Know:

Today I Am Affirming: I Know I Am Worthy Of:

What Do I Believe I Will Need Help With Today?   Today I Want To Release:

What Will I Do Today That Will Help Me To Feel Happy & Relaxed? Today I Am Reclaiming:

ACT ONE: IT TRIED TO DESTROY ME

NIGHTLY THOUGHTS

How Do I Currently Feel And Why Do I Feel This Way?

Tomorrow I Look Forward To:

Today's Breakup Symptoms:

Did My Ex Try To Get My Attention In Any Way Today?

Today I Learned:

If I Responded Yes To The Previous Prompt, Explain How:

Today I Was Tempted To:

Did I Do A Good Job Today Of Protecting My Peace And Space?

Did I Act On The Thing I Was Tempted To Do? If So, Why Did I Give In To It, And What Were The Results Of My Actions?

What Could I Have Done A Better Job With Today?

What Did I Tell My Ex Today, And If I Didn't Speak To Them, What Would I Want To Tell My Ex?

Tatiana's Personal Note: You Can Have And Be Anything. Choose To Be A Believer In Yourself.

ACT ONE: IT TRIED TO DESTROY ME

MORNING THOUGHTS

Date: Mood:

I Woke Up Feeling: Today I Will Intentionally Focus On:

Did I Wake Up Today Feeling Better Than I Did Yesterday?   Today I Want God To Know:

Today I Am Affirming: I Know I Am Worthy Of:

What Do I Believe I Will Need Help With Today?   Today I Want To Release:

What Will I Do Today That Will Help Me To Feel Happy & Relaxed?   Today I Am Reclaiming:

ACT ONE: IT TRIED TO DESTROY ME

NIGHTLY THOUGHTS

How Do I Currently Feel And Why Do I Feel This Way?

Did My Ex Try To Get My Attention In Any Way Today?

If I Responded Yes To The Previous Prompt, Explain How:

Did I Do A Good Job Today Of Protecting My Peace And Space?

What Could I Have Done A Better Job With Today?

Tomorrow I Look Forward To:

Today's Breakup Symptoms:

Today I Learned:

Today I Was Tempted To:

Did I Act On The Thing I Was Tempted To Do? If So, Why Did I Give In To It, And What Were The Results Of My Actions?

What Did I Tell My Ex Today, And If I Didn't Speak To Them, What Would I Want To Tell My Ex?

Tatiana's Personal Note: Know What You Deserve.

ACT ONE: IT TRIED TO DESTROY ME

MORNING THOUGHTS

Date: Mood:

I Woke Up Feeling: Today I Will Intentionally Focus On:

Did I Wake Up Today Feeling Better Than I Did Yesterday?   Today I Want God To Know:

Today I Am Affirming: I Know I Am Worthy Of:

What Do I Believe I Will Need Help With Today?   Today I Want To Release:

What Will I Do Today That Will Help Me To Feel Happy & Relaxed? Today I Am Reclaiming:

ACT ONE: IT TRIED TO DESTROY ME

NIGHTLY THOUGHTS

How Do I Currently Feel And Why Do I Feel This Way?

Did My Ex Try To Get My Attention In Any Way Today?

If I Responded Yes To The Previous Prompt, Explain How:

Did I Do A Good Job Today Of Protecting My Peace And Space?

What Could I Have Done A Better Job With Today?

Tomorrow I Look Forward To:

Today's Breakup Symptoms:

Today I Learned:

Today I Was Tempted To:

Did I Act On The Thing I Was Tempted To Do? If So, Why Did I Give In To It, And What Were The Results Of My Actions?

What Did I Tell My Ex Today, And If I Didn't Speak To Them, What Would I Want To Tell My Ex?

Tatiana's Personal Note: It Is Okay To Make Mistakes. Be Sure To Grow From Them.

ACT ONE: IT TRIED TO DESTROY ME

MORNING THOUGHTS

Date: Mood:

I Woke Up Feeling: Today I Will Intentionally Focus On:

Did I Wake Up Today Feeling Better Than I Did   Today I Want God To Know:
Yesterday?

Today I Am Affirming: I Know I Am Worthy Of:

What Do I Believe I Will Need Help With   Today I Want To Release:
Today?

What Will I Do Today That Will Help Me To   Today I Am Reclaiming:
Feel Happy & Relaxed?

ACT ONE: IT TRIED TO DESTROY ME

NIGHTLY THOUGHTS

How Do I Currently Feel And Why Do I Feel This Way?

Did My Ex Try To Get My Attention In Any Way Today?

If I Responded Yes To The Previous Prompt, Explain How:

Did I Do A Good Job Today Of Protecting My Peace And Space?

What Could I Have Done A Better Job With Today?

Tomorrow I Look Forward To:

Today's Breakup Symptoms:

Today I Learned:

Today I Was Tempted To:

Did I Act On The Thing I Was Tempted To Do? If So, Why Did I Give In To It, And What Were The Results Of My Actions?

What Did I Tell My Ex Today, And If I Didn't Speak To Them, What Would I Want To Tell My Ex?

Tatiana's Personal Note: Love When You Are Hurting. Love When You Are Happy.

ACT ONE: IT TRIED TO DESTROY ME

MORNING THOUGHTS

Date: Mood:

I Woke Up Feeling: Today I Will Intentionally Focus On:

Did I Wake Up Today Feeling Better Than I Did Yesterday?   Today I Want God To Know:

Today I Am Affirming: I Know I Am Worthy Of:

What Do I Believe I Will Need Help With Today?   Today I Want To Release:

What Will I Do Today That Will Help Me To Feel Happy & Relaxed?   Today I Am Reclaiming:

ACT ONE: IT TRIED TO DESTROY ME

NIGHTLY THOUGHTS

How Do I Currently Feel And Why Do I Feel This Way?	Tomorrow I Look Forward To:
	Today's Breakup Symptoms:
Did My Ex Try To Get My Attention In Any Way Today?	
	Today I Learned:
If I Responded Yes To The Previous Prompt, Explain How:	
	Today I Was Tempted To:
Did I Do A Good Job Today Of Protecting My Peace And Space?	Did I Act On The Thing I Was Tempted To Do? If So, Why Did I Give In To It, And What Were The Results Of My Actions?
What Could I Have Done A Better Job With Today?	What Did I Tell My Ex Today, And If I Didn't Speak To Them, What Would I Want To Tell My Ex?

Tatiana's Personal Note: It Is How You Deal With Your Imperfections That Makes You Perfect.

ACT ONE: IT TRIED TO DESTROY ME

MORNING THOUGHTS

Date: Mood:

I Woke Up Feeling: Today I Will Intentionally Focus On:

Did I Wake Up Today Feeling Better Than I Did Yesterday?   Today I Want God To Know:

Today I Am Affirming: I Know I Am Worthy Of:

What Do I Believe I Will Need Help With Today?   Today I Want To Release:

What Will I Do Today That Will Help Me To Feel Happy & Relaxed?   Today I Am Reclaiming:

ACT ONE: IT TRIED TO DESTROY ME

NIGHTLY THOUGHTS

How Do I Currently Feel And Why Do I Feel This Way?

Tomorrow I Look Forward To:

Today's Breakup Symptoms:

Did My Ex Try To Get My Attention In Any Way Today?

Today I Learned:

If I Responded Yes To The Previous Prompt, Explain How:

Today I Was Tempted To:

Did I Do A Good Job Today Of Protecting My Peace And Space?

Did I Act On The Thing I Was Tempted To Do? If So, Why Did I Give In To It, And What Were The Results Of My Actions?

What Could I Have Done A Better Job With Today?

What Did I Tell My Ex Today, And If I Didn't Speak To Them, What Would I Want To Tell My Ex?

Tatiana's Personal Note: Never Feel Guilty For Doing What's Best For You.

MY HEART MAY BE HURTING, BUT IT IS FORGIVING.

**EVERYTHING
IS FALLING INTO PLACE.
EVERYTHING.**

ACT ONE: IT TRIED TO DESTROY ME

MORNING THOUGHTS

Date: Mood:

I Woke Up Feeling: Today I Will Intentionally Focus On:

Did I Wake Up Today Feeling Better Than I Did   Today I Want God To Know:
Yesterday?

Today I Am Affirming: I Know I Am Worthy Of:

What Do I Believe I Will Need Help With   Today I Want To Release:
Today?

What Will I Do Today That Will Help Me To   Today I Am Reclaiming:
Feel Happy & Relaxed?

ACT ONE: IT TRIED TO DESTROY ME

NIGHTLY THOUGHTS

How Do I Currently Feel And Why Do I Feel This Way?

Did My Ex Try To Get My Attention In Any Way Today?

If I Responded Yes To The Previous Prompt, Explain How:

Did I Do A Good Job Today Of Protecting My Peace And Space?

What Could I Have Done A Better Job With Today?

Tomorrow I Look Forward To:

Today's Breakup Symptoms:

Today I Learned:

Today I Was Tempted To:

Did I Act On The Thing I Was Tempted To Do? If So, Why Did I Give In To It, And What Were The Results Of My Actions?

What Did I Tell My Ex Today, And If I Didn't Speak To Them, What Would I Want To Tell My Ex?

Tatiana's Personal Note: What You Overcome Is What Brings You Closer To Who You Have Prayed To Become.

ACT ONE: IT TRIED TO DESTROY ME

MORNING THOUGHTS

Date: Mood:

I Woke Up Feeling: Today I Will Intentionally Focus On:

Did I Wake Up Today Feeling Better Than I Did   Today I Want God To Know:
Yesterday?

Today I Am Affirming: I Know I Am Worthy Of:

What Do I Believe I Will Need Help With   Today I Want To Release:
Today?

What Will I Do Today That Will Help Me To   Today I Am Reclaiming:
Feel Happy & Relaxed?

ACT ONE: IT TRIED TO DESTROY ME

NIGHTLY THOUGHTS

How Do I Currently Feel And Why Do I Feel This Way?

Did My Ex Try To Get My Attention In Any Way Today?

If I Responded Yes To The Previous Prompt, Explain How:

Did I Do A Good Job Today Of Protecting My Peace And Space?

What Could I Have Done A Better Job With Today?

Tomorrow I Look Forward To:

Today's Breakup Symptoms:

Today I Learned:

Today I Was Tempted To:

Did I Act On The Thing I Was Tempted To Do? If So, Why Did I Give In To It, And What Were The Results Of My Actions?

What Did I Tell My Ex Today, And If I Didn't Speak To Them, What Would I Want To Tell My Ex?

Tatiana's Personal Note: You Are Beauty.

ACT ONE: IT TRIED TO DESTROY ME

MORNING THOUGHTS

Date: Mood:

I Woke Up Feeling: Today I Will Intentionally Focus On:

Did I Wake Up Today Feeling Better Than I Did   Today I Want God To Know:
Yesterday?

Today I Am Affirming: I Know I Am Worthy Of:

What Do I Believe I Will Need Help With   Today I Want To Release:
Today?

What Will I Do Today That Will Help Me To   Today I Am Reclaiming:
Feel Happy & Relaxed?

ACT ONE: IT TRIED TO DESTROY ME

NIGHTLY THOUGHTS

How Do I Currently Feel And Why Do I Feel This Way?

Tomorrow I Look Forward To:

Today's Breakup Symptoms:

Did My Ex Try To Get My Attention In Any Way Today?

Today I Learned:

If I Responded Yes To The Previous Prompt, Explain How:

Today I Was Tempted To:

Did I Do A Good Job Today Of Protecting My Peace And Space?

Did I Act On The Thing I Was Tempted To Do? If So, Why Did I Give In To It, And What Were The Results Of My Actions?

What Could I Have Done A Better Job With Today?

What Did I Tell My Ex Today, And If I Didn't Speak To Them, What Would I Want To Tell My Ex?

Tatiana's Personal Note: Stillness Will Eliminate Confusion.

ACT ONE: IT TRIED TO DESTROY ME

MORNING THOUGHTS

Date: Mood:

I Woke Up Feeling: Today I Will Intentionally Focus On:

Did I Wake Up Today Feeling Better Than I Did Yesterday? Today I Want God To Know:

Today I Am Affirming: I Know I Am Worthy Of:

What Do I Believe I Will Need Help With Today?   Today I Want To Release:

What Will I Do Today That Will Help Me To Feel Happy & Relaxed?   Today I Am Reclaiming:

ACT ONE: IT TRIED TO DESTROY ME

NIGHTLY THOUGHTS

How Do I Currently Feel And Why Do I Feel This Way?

Did My Ex Try To Get My Attention In Any Way Today?

If I Responded Yes To The Previous Prompt, Explain How:

Did I Do A Good Job Today Of Protecting My Peace And Space?

What Could I Have Done A Better Job With Today?

Tomorrow I Look Forward To:

Today's Breakup Symptoms:

Today I Learned:

Today I Was Tempted To:

Did I Act On The Thing I Was Tempted To Do? If So, Why Did I Give In To It, And What Were The Results Of My Actions?

What Did I Tell My Ex Today, And If I Didn't Speak To Them, What Would I Want To Tell My Ex?

Tatiana's Personal Note: Sometimes You Go Through The Worst Times Of Your Life To Get To The Best Times.

ACT ONE: IT TRIED TO DESTROY ME

MORNING THOUGHTS

Date: Mood:

I Woke Up Feeling: Today I Will Intentionally Focus On:

Did I Wake Up Today Feeling Better Than I Did Yesterday?   Today I Want God To Know:

Today I Am Affirming: I Know I Am Worthy Of:

What Do I Believe I Will Need Help With Today? Today I Want To Release:

What Will I Do Today That Will Help Me To Feel Happy & Relaxed?   Today I Am Reclaiming:

ACT ONE: IT TRIED TO DESTROY ME
NIGHTLY THOUGHTS

How Do I Currently Feel And Why Do I Feel This Way?

Did My Ex Try To Get My Attention In Any Way Today?

If I Responded Yes To The Previous Prompt, Explain How:

Did I Do A Good Job Today Of Protecting My Peace And Space?

What Could I Have Done A Better Job With Today?

Tomorrow I Look Forward To:

Today's Breakup Symptoms:

Today I Learned:

Today I Was Tempted To:

Did I Act On The Thing I Was Tempted To Do? If So, Why Did I Give In To It, And What Were The Results Of My Actions?

What Did I Tell My Ex Today, And If I Didn't Speak To Them, What Would I Want To Tell My Ex?

Tatiana's Personal Note: Broken Hearts Do Not Last Forever.

ACT ONE: IT TRIED TO DESTROY ME

MORNING THOUGHTS

Date: Mood:

I Woke Up Feeling: Today I Will Intentionally Focus On:

Did I Wake Up Today Feeling Better Than I Did Yesterday?   Today I Want God To Know:

Today I Am Affirming: I Know I Am Worthy Of:

What Do I Believe I Will Need Help With Today?   Today I Want To Release:

What Will I Do Today That Will Help Me To Feel Happy & Relaxed?   Today I Am Reclaiming:

ACT ONE: IT TRIED TO DESTROY ME

NIGHTLY THOUGHTS

How Do I Currently Feel And Why Do I Feel This Way?	Tomorrow I Look Forward To:
	Today's Breakup Symptoms:
Did My Ex Try To Get My Attention In Any Way Today?	
	Today I Learned:
If I Responded Yes To The Previous Prompt, Explain How:	
	Today I Was Tempted To:
Did I Do A Good Job Today Of Protecting My Peace And Space?	Did I Act On The Thing I Was Tempted To Do? If So, Why Did I Give In To It, And What Were The Results Of My Actions?
What Could I Have Done A Better Job With Today?	What Did I Tell My Ex Today, And If I Didn't Speak To Them, What Would I Want To Tell My Ex?

Tatiana's Personal Note: The Breakup Was A Set Up For A Breakthrough.

ACT ONE: IT TRIED TO DESTROY ME

MORNING THOUGHTS

Date: Mood:

I Woke Up Feeling: Today I Will Intentionally Focus On:

Did I Wake Up Today Feeling Better Than I Did Yesterday?   Today I Want God To Know:

Today I Am Affirming: I Know I Am Worthy Of:

What Do I Believe I Will Need Help With Today?   Today I Want To Release:

What Will I Do Today That Will Help Me To Feel Happy & Relaxed?   Today I Am Reclaiming:

ACT ONE: IT TRIED TO DESTROY ME

NIGHTLY THOUGHTS

How Do I Currently Feel And Why Do I Feel This Way?

Tomorrow I Look Forward To:

Today's Breakup Symptoms:

Did My Ex Try To Get My Attention In Any Way Today?

Today I Learned:

If I Responded Yes To The Previous Prompt, Explain How:

Today I Was Tempted To:

Did I Do A Good Job Today Of Protecting My Peace And Space?

Did I Act On The Thing I Was Tempted To Do? If So, Why Did I Give In To It, And What Were The Results Of My Actions?

What Could I Have Done A Better Job With Today?

What Did I Tell My Ex Today, And If I Didn't Speak To Them, What Would I Want To Tell My Ex?

Tatiana's Personal Note: Sometimes The Person Who You Think Deserves You Doesn't.

GOD IS GETTING YOU THROUGH IT.

SHE LET GO OF WHAT COULD NOT PRESERVE HER AND REPLACED IT WITH WHAT FORTIFIED HER.

ACT ONE: IT TRIED TO DESTROY ME

MORNING THOUGHTS

Date: Mood:

I Woke Up Feeling: Today I Will Intentionally Focus On:

Did I Wake Up Today Feeling Better Than I Did Yesterday?   Today I Want God To Know:

Today I Am Affirming: I Know I Am Worthy Of:

What Do I Believe I Will Need Help With Today?   Today I Want To Release:

What Will I Do Today That Will Help Me To Feel Happy & Relaxed?   Today I Am Reclaiming:

ACT ONE: IT TRIED TO DESTROY ME
NIGHTLY THOUGHTS

How Do I Currently Feel And Why Do I Feel This Way?

Did My Ex Try To Get My Attention In Any Way Today?

If I Responded Yes To The Previous Prompt, Explain How:

Did I Do A Good Job Today Of Protecting My Peace And Space?

What Could I Have Done A Better Job With Today?

Tomorrow I Look Forward To:

Today's Breakup Symptoms:

Today I Learned:

Today I Was Tempted To:

Did I Act On The Thing I Was Tempted To Do? If So, Why Did I Give In To It, And What Were The Results Of My Actions?

What Did I Tell My Ex Today, And If I Didn't Speak To Them, What Would I Want To Tell My Ex?

Tatiana's Personal Note: What Has Left Is Not Better Than What Is Coming.

ACT ONE: IT TRIED TO DESTROY ME

MORNING THOUGHTS

Date: Mood:

I Woke Up Feeling: Today I Will Intentionally Focus On:

Did I Wake Up Today Feeling Better Than I Did   Today I Want God To Know:
Yesterday?

Today I Am Affirming: I Know I Am Worthy Of:

What Do I Believe I Will Need Help With   Today I Want To Release:
Today?

What Will I Do Today That Will Help Me To   Today I Am Reclaiming:
Feel Happy & Relaxed?

ACT ONE: IT TRIED TO DESTROY ME

NIGHTLY THOUGHTS

How Do I Currently Feel And Why Do I Feel This Way?

Did My Ex Try To Get My Attention In Any Way Today?

If I Responded Yes To The Previous Prompt, Explain How:

Did I Do A Good Job Today Of Protecting My Peace And Space?

What Could I Have Done A Better Job With Today?

Tomorrow I Look Forward To:

Today's Breakup Symptoms:

Today I Learned:

Today I Was Tempted To:

Did I Act On The Thing I Was Tempted To Do? If So, Why Did I Give In To It, And What Were The Results Of My Actions?

What Did I Tell My Ex Today, And If I Didn't Speak To Them, What Would I Want To Tell My Ex?

Tatiana's Personal Note: She Believed So Much That It Came To Life. So Now They Believe.

ACT ONE: IT TRIED TO DESTROY ME

MORNING THOUGHTS

Date: Mood:

I Woke Up Feeling: | Today I Will Intentionally Focus On:

Did I Wake Up Today Feeling Better Than I Did Yesterday? | Today I Want God To Know:

Today I Am Affirming: | I Know I Am Worthy Of:

What Do I Believe I Will Need Help With Today? | Today I Want To Release:

What Will I Do Today That Will Help Me To Feel Happy & Relaxed? | Today I Am Reclaiming:

ACT ONE: IT TRIED TO DESTROY ME

NIGHTLY THOUGHTS

How Do I Currently Feel And Why Do I Feel This Way?

Tomorrow I Look Forward To:

Today's Breakup Symptoms:

Did My Ex Try To Get My Attention In Any Way Today?

Today I Learned:

If I Responded Yes To The Previous Prompt, Explain How:

Today I Was Tempted To:

Did I Do A Good Job Today Of Protecting My Peace And Space?

Did I Act On The Thing I Was Tempted To Do? If So, Why Did I Give In To It, And What Were The Results Of My Actions?

What Could I Have Done A Better Job With Today?

What Did I Tell My Ex Today, And If I Didn't Speak To Them, What Would I Want To Tell My Ex?

Tatiana's Personal Note: True Strength Is Knowing When To Walk Away From Nonsense.

ACT ONE: IT TRIED TO DESTROY ME

MORNING THOUGHTS

Date: Mood:

I Woke Up Feeling: Today I Will Intentionally Focus On:

Did I Wake Up Today Feeling Better Than I Did Yesterday?   Today I Want God To Know:

Today I Am Affirming: I Know I Am Worthy Of:

What Do I Believe I Will Need Help With Today?   Today I Want To Release:

What Will I Do Today That Will Help Me To Feel Happy & Relaxed?   Today I Am Reclaiming:

ACT ONE: IT TRIED TO DESTROY ME

NIGHTLY THOUGHTS

How Do I Currently Feel And Why Do I Feel This Way?

Did My Ex Try To Get My Attention In Any Way Today?

If I Responded Yes To The Previous Prompt, Explain How:

Did I Do A Good Job Today Of Protecting My Peace And Space?

What Could I Have Done A Better Job With Today?

Tomorrow I Look Forward To:

Today's Breakup Symptoms:

Today I Learned:

Today I Was Tempted To:

Did I Act On The Thing I Was Tempted To Do? If So, Why Did I Give In To It, And What Were The Results Of My Actions?

What Did I Tell My Ex Today, And If I Didn't Speak To Them, What Would I Want To Tell My Ex?

Tatiana's Personal Note: You Are Not Just Standing Up For Yourself. You Are Standing Up For All Those Who Are Watching You.

ACT ONE: IT TRIED TO DESTROY ME

MORNING THOUGHTS

Date: Mood:

I Woke Up Feeling: Today I Will Intentionally Focus On:

Did I Wake Up Today Feeling Better Than I Did Yesterday? | Today I Want God To Know:

Today I Am Affirming: I Know I Am Worthy Of:

What Do I Believe I Will Need Help With Today?   Today I Want To Release:

What Will I Do Today That Will Help Me To Feel Happy & Relaxed? | Today I Am Reclaiming:

ACT ONE: IT TRIED TO DESTROY ME

NIGHTLY THOUGHTS

How Do I Currently Feel And Why Do I Feel This Way?

Did My Ex Try To Get My Attention In Any Way Today?

If I Responded Yes To The Previous Prompt, Explain How:

Did I Do A Good Job Today Of Protecting My Peace And Space?

What Could I Have Done A Better Job With Today?

Tomorrow I Look Forward To:

Today's Breakup Symptoms:

Today I Learned:

Today I Was Tempted To:

Did I Act On The Thing I Was Tempted To Do? If So, Why Did I Give In To It, And What Were The Results Of My Actions?

What Did I Tell My Ex Today, And If I Didn't Speak To Them, What Would I Want To Tell My Ex?

Tatiana's Personal Note: You Are Everything To Somebody.

MY LIFE CHANGED WHEN I DECIDED TO BE HAPPY.... AGAIN.

NO MORE UNHEALTHY ATTACHMENTS.

ACT ONE: IT TRIED TO DESTROY ME

MORNING THOUGHTS

Date: Mood:

I Woke Up Feeling: Today I Will Intentionally Focus On:

Did I Wake Up Today Feeling Better Than I Did Yesterday?   Today I Want God To Know:

Today I Am Affirming: I Know I Am Worthy Of:

What Do I Believe I Will Need Help With Today?   Today I Want To Release:

What Will I Do Today That Will Help Me To Feel Happy & Relaxed?   Today I Am Reclaiming:

ACT ONE: IT TRIED TO DESTROY ME

NIGHTLY THOUGHTS

How Do I Currently Feel And Why Do I Feel This Way?

Tomorrow I Look Forward To:

Today's Breakup Symptoms:

Did My Ex Try To Get My Attention In Any Way Today?

Today I Learned:

If I Responded Yes To The Previous Prompt, Explain How:

Today I Was Tempted To:

Did I Do A Good Job Today Of Protecting My Peace And Space?

Did I Act On The Thing I Was Tempted To Do? If So, Why Did I Give In To It, And What Were The Results Of My Actions?

What Could I Have Done A Better Job With Today?

What Did I Tell My Ex Today, And If I Didn't Speak To Them, What Would I Want To Tell My Ex?

Tatiana's Personal Note: Let Love Guide Your Life. Not Hurt.

ACT ONE: IT TRIED TO DESTROY ME

MORNING THOUGHTS

Date: Mood:

I Woke Up Feeling: Today I Will Intentionally Focus On:

Did I Wake Up Today Feeling Better Than I Did Yesterday?   Today I Want God To Know:

Today I Am Affirming: I Know I Am Worthy Of:

What Do I Believe I Will Need Help With Today?   Today I Want To Release:

What Will I Do Today That Will Help Me To Feel Happy & Relaxed?   Today I Am Reclaiming:

ACT ONE: IT TRIED TO DESTROY ME

NIGHTLY THOUGHTS

How Do I Currently Feel And Why Do I Feel This Way?

Did My Ex Try To Get My Attention In Any Way Today?

If I Responded Yes To The Previous Prompt, Explain How:

Did I Do A Good Job Today Of Protecting My Peace And Space?

What Could I Have Done A Better Job With Today?

Tomorrow I Look Forward To:

Today's Breakup Symptoms:

Today I Learned:

Today I Was Tempted To:

Did I Act On The Thing I Was Tempted To Do? If So, Why Did I Give In To It, And What Were The Results Of My Actions?

What Did I Tell My Ex Today, And If I Didn't Speak To Them, What Would I Want To Tell My Ex?

Tatiana's Personal Note: Always Believe In You.

ACT ONE: IT TRIED TO DESTROY ME

MORNING THOUGHTS

Date: Mood:

I Woke Up Feeling: Today I Will Intentionally Focus On:

Did I Wake Up Today Feeling Better Than I Did Yesterday?   Today I Want God To Know:

Today I Am Affirming: I Know I Am Worthy Of:

What Do I Believe I Will Need Help With Today?   Today I Want To Release:

What Will I Do Today That Will Help Me To Feel Happy & Relaxed?   Today I Am Reclaiming:

ACT ONE: IT TRIED TO DESTROY ME
NIGHTLY THOUGHTS

How Do I Currently Feel And Why Do I Feel This Way?

Did My Ex Try To Get My Attention In Any Way Today?

If I Responded Yes To The Previous Prompt, Explain How:

Did I Do A Good Job Today Of Protecting My Peace And Space?

What Could I Have Done A Better Job With Today?

Tomorrow I Look Forward To:

Today's Breakup Symptoms:

Today I Learned:

Today I Was Tempted To:

Did I Act On The Thing I Was Tempted To Do? If So, Why Did I Give In To It, And What Were The Results Of My Actions?

What Did I Tell My Ex Today, And If I Didn't Speak To Them, What Would I Want To Tell My Ex?

Tatiana's Personal Note: Remember That The Ones Who Criticize You Are Not Perfect.

ACT ONE: IT TRIED TO DESTROY ME

MORNING THOUGHTS

Date:	Mood:

I Woke Up Feeling:

Today I Will Intentionally Focus On:

Did I Wake Up Today Feeling Better Than I Did Yesterday?

Today I Want God To Know:

Today I Am Affirming:

I Know I Am Worthy Of:

What Do I Believe I Will Need Help With Today?

Today I Want To Release:

What Will I Do Today That Will Help Me To Feel Happy & Relaxed?

Today I Am Reclaiming:

ACT ONE: IT TRIED TO DESTROY ME

NIGHTLY THOUGHTS

How Do I Currently Feel And Why Do I Feel This Way?

Did My Ex Try To Get My Attention In Any Way Today?

If I Responded Yes To The Previous Prompt, Explain How:

Did I Do A Good Job Today Of Protecting My Peace And Space?

What Could I Have Done A Better Job With Today?

Tomorrow I Look Forward To:

Today's Breakup Symptoms:

Today I Learned:

Today I Was Tempted To:

Did I Act On The Thing I Was Tempted To Do? If So, Why Did I Give In To It, And What Were The Results Of My Actions?

What Did I Tell My Ex Today, And If I Didn't Speak To Them, What Would I Want To Tell My Ex?

Tatiana's Personal Note: There is Peace After The Storm. Focus On The Peace.

ACT ONE: IT TRIED TO DESTROY ME

MORNING THOUGHTS

Date: Mood:

I Woke Up Feeling: Today I Will Intentionally Focus On:

Did I Wake Up Today Feeling Better Than I Did Yesterday?   Today I Want God To Know:

Today I Am Affirming: I Know I Am Worthy Of:

What Do I Believe I Will Need Help With Today?   Today I Want To Release:

What Will I Do Today That Will Help Me To Feel Happy & Relaxed?   Today I Am Reclaiming:

ACT ONE: IT TRIED TO DESTROY ME

NIGHTLY THOUGHTS

How Do I Currently Feel And Why Do I Feel This Way?

Tomorrow I Look Forward To:

Today's Breakup Symptoms:

Did My Ex Try To Get My Attention In Any Way Today?

Today I Learned:

If I Responded Yes To The Previous Prompt, Explain How:

Today I Was Tempted To:

Did I Do A Good Job Today Of Protecting My Peace And Space?

Did I Act On The Thing I Was Tempted To Do? If So, Why Did I Give In To It, And What Were The Results Of My Actions?

What Could I Have Done A Better Job With Today?

What Did I Tell My Ex Today, And If I Didn't Speak To Them, What Would I Want To Tell My Ex?

Tatiana's Personal Note: Your Future Does Not Have To Look Like Your Past.

YOU DO NOT UNDERSTAND
WHAT I AM DOING NOW,
BUT SOMEDAY YOU WILL.
-GOD

MY HEART IS GOLD.
I'M WORTH IT.

ACT ONE: IT TRIED TO DESTROY ME

MORNING THOUGHTS

Date: Mood:

I Woke Up Feeling: Today I Will Intentionally Focus On:

Did I Wake Up Today Feeling Better Than I Did   Today I Want God To Know:
Yesterday?

Today I Am Affirming: I Know I Am Worthy Of:

What Do I Believe I Will Need Help With   Today I Want To Release:
Today?

What Will I Do Today That Will Help Me To   Today I Am Reclaiming:
Feel Happy & Relaxed?

ACT ONE: IT TRIED TO DESTROY ME
NIGHTLY THOUGHTS

How Do I Currently Feel And Why Do I Feel This Way?	Tomorrow I Look Forward To:
Did My Ex Try To Get My Attention In Any Way Today?	Today's Breakup Symptoms:
	Today I Learned:
If I Responded Yes To The Previous Prompt, Explain How:	Today I Was Tempted To:
Did I Do A Good Job Today Of Protecting My Peace And Space?	Did I Act On The Thing I Was Tempted To Do? If So, Why Did I Give In To It, And What Were The Results Of My Actions?
What Could I Have Done A Better Job With Today?	What Did I Tell My Ex Today, And If I Didn't Speak To Them, What Would I Want To Tell My Ex?

Tatiana's Personal Note: You Don't Have To Pretend It Doesn't Hurt. You Just Have To Leave What Hurts You Alone.

ACT ONE: IT TRIED TO DESTROY ME

MORNING THOUGHTS

Date: Mood:

I Woke Up Feeling: Today I Will Intentionally Focus On:

Did I Wake Up Today Feeling Better Than I Did Yesterday?   Today I Want God To Know:

Today I Am Affirming: I Know I Am Worthy Of:

What Do I Believe I Will Need Help With Today?   Today I Want To Release:

What Will I Do Today That Will Help Me To Feel Happy & Relaxed?   Today I Am Reclaiming:

ACT ONE: IT TRIED TO DESTROY ME

NIGHTLY THOUGHTS

How Do I Currently Feel And Why Do I Feel This Way?

Did My Ex Try To Get My Attention In Any Way Today?

If I Responded Yes To The Previous Prompt, Explain How:

Did I Do A Good Job Today Of Protecting My Peace And Space?

What Could I Have Done A Better Job With Today?

Tomorrow I Look Forward To:

Today's Breakup Symptoms:

Today I Learned:

Today I Was Tempted To:

Did I Act On The Thing I Was Tempted To Do? If So, Why Did I Give In To It, And What Were The Results Of My Actions?

What Did I Tell My Ex Today, And If I Didn't Speak To Them, What Would I Want To Tell My Ex?

==Tatiana's Personal Note: Your Next Blessing Can Show Up At Anytime.==

ACT ONE: IT TRIED TO DESTROY ME

MORNING THOUGHTS

Date: Mood:

I Woke Up Feeling: Today I Will Intentionally Focus On:

Did I Wake Up Today Feeling Better Than I Did Yesterday?   Today I Want God To Know:

Today I Am Affirming: I Know I Am Worthy Of:

What Do I Believe I Will Need Help With Today?   Today I Want To Release:

What Will I Do Today That Will Help Me To Feel Happy & Relaxed?   Today I Am Reclaiming:

ACT ONE: IT TRIED TO DESTROY ME

NIGHTLY THOUGHTS

How Do I Currently Feel And Why Do I Feel This Way?

Tomorrow I Look Forward To:

Today's Breakup Symptoms:

Did My Ex Try To Get My Attention In Any Way Today?

Today I Learned:

If I Responded Yes To The Previous Prompt, Explain How:

Today I Was Tempted To:

Did I Do A Good Job Today Of Protecting My Peace And Space?

Did I Act On The Thing I Was Tempted To Do? If So, Why Did I Give In To It, And What Were The Results Of My Actions?

What Could I Have Done A Better Job With Today?

What Did I Tell My Ex Today, And If I Didn't Speak To Them, What Would I Want To Tell My Ex?

Tatiana's Personal Note: Prepare For The Woman You Want To Be.

I'VE GOT THIS.

I AM MY BIGGEST PRIORITY.

ACT ONE: IT TRIED TO DESTROY ME

MORNING THOUGHTS

Date: Mood:

I Woke Up Feeling: Today I Will Intentionally Focus On:

Did I Wake Up Today Feeling Better Than I Did Yesterday?   Today I Want God To Know:

Today I Am Affirming: I Know I Am Worthy Of:

What Do I Believe I Will Need Help With Today?   Today I Want To Release:

What Will I Do Today That Will Help Me To Feel Happy & Relaxed?   Today I Am Reclaiming:

ACT ONE: IT TRIED TO DESTROY ME
NIGHTLY THOUGHTS

How Do I Currently Feel And Why Do I Feel This Way?

Did My Ex Try To Get My Attention In Any Way Today?

If I Responded Yes To The Previous Prompt, Explain How:

Did I Do A Good Job Today Of Protecting My Peace And Space?

What Could I Have Done A Better Job With Today?

Tomorrow I Look Forward To:

Today's Breakup Symptoms:

Today I Learned:

Today I Was Tempted To:

Did I Act On The Thing I Was Tempted To Do? If So, Why Did I Give In To It, And What Were The Results Of My Actions?

What Did I Tell My Ex Today, And If I Didn't Speak To Them, What Would I Want To Tell My Ex?

Tatiana's Personal Note: Don't Know What To Ask God For? Pray About That.

ACT ONE: IT TRIED TO DESTROY ME

MORNING THOUGHTS

Date: Mood:

I Woke Up Feeling: Today I Will Intentionally Focus On:

Did I Wake Up Today Feeling Better Than I Did Yesterday?   Today I Want God To Know:

Today I Am Affirming: I Know I Am Worthy Of:

What Do I Believe I Will Need Help With Today? Today I Want To Release:

What Will I Do Today That Will Help Me To Feel Happy & Relaxed?   Today I Am Reclaiming:

ACT ONE: IT TRIED TO DESTROY ME

NIGHTLY THOUGHTS

How Do I Currently Feel And Why Do I Feel This Way?

Did My Ex Try To Get My Attention In Any Way Today?

If I Responded Yes To The Previous Prompt, Explain How:

Did I Do A Good Job Today Of Protecting My Peace And Space?

What Could I Have Done A Better Job With Today?

Tomorrow I Look Forward To:

Today's Breakup Symptoms:

Today I Learned:

Today I Was Tempted To:

Did I Act On The Thing I Was Tempted To Do? If So, Why Did I Give In To It, And What Were The Results Of My Actions?

What Did I Tell My Ex Today, And If I Didn't Speak To Them, What Would I Want To Tell My Ex?

Tatiana's Personal Note: Just Because It Did Not Work Out Does Not Mean There Is Something Wrong With You.

ACT ONE: IT TRIED TO DESTROY ME

MORNING THOUGHTS

Date: Mood:

I Woke Up Feeling: Today I Will Intentionally Focus On:

Did I Wake Up Today Feeling Better Than I Did Yesterday?   Today I Want God To Know:

Today I Am Affirming: I Know I Am Worthy Of:

What Do I Believe I Will Need Help With Today?   Today I Want To Release:

What Will I Do Today That Will Help Me To Feel Happy & Relaxed?   Today I Am Reclaiming:

ACT ONE: IT TRIED TO DESTROY ME

NIGHTLY THOUGHTS

How Do I Currently Feel And Why Do I Feel This Way?

Tomorrow I Look Forward To:

Today's Breakup Symptoms:

Did My Ex Try To Get My Attention In Any Way Today?

Today I Learned:

If I Responded Yes To The Previous Prompt, Explain How:

Today I Was Tempted To:

Did I Do A Good Job Today Of Protecting My Peace And Space?

Did I Act On The Thing I Was Tempted To Do? If So, Why Did I Give In To It, And What Were The Results Of My Actions?

What Could I Have Done A Better Job With Today?

What Did I Tell My Ex Today, And If I Didn't Speak To Them, What Would I Want To Tell My Ex?

Tatiana's Personal Note: Always Speak Great Things About You. Your Spirit Is Listening.

ACT ONE: IT TRIED TO DESTROY ME

MORNING THOUGHTS

Date: Mood:

I Woke Up Feeling: Today I Will Intentionally Focus On:

Did I Wake Up Today Feeling Better Than I Did Yesterday?   Today I Want God To Know:

Today I Am Affirming: I Know I Am Worthy Of:

What Do I Believe I Will Need Help With Today?   Today I Want To Release:

What Will I Do Today That Will Help Me To Feel Happy & Relaxed?   Today I Am Reclaiming:

ACT ONE: IT TRIED TO DESTROY ME

NIGHTLY THOUGHTS

How Do I Currently Feel And Why Do I Feel This Way?

Did My Ex Try To Get My Attention In Any Way Today?

If I Responded Yes To The Previous Prompt, Explain How:

Did I Do A Good Job Today Of Protecting My Peace And Space?

What Could I Have Done A Better Job With Today?

Tomorrow I Look Forward To:

Today's Breakup Symptoms:

Today I Learned:

Today I Was Tempted To:

Did I Act On The Thing I Was Tempted To Do? If So, Why Did I Give In To It, And What Were The Results Of My Actions?

What Did I Tell My Ex Today, And If I Didn't Speak To Them, What Would I Want To Tell My Ex?

Tatiana's Personal Note: Be Your Favorite Person.

MY OPINIONS, FEELINGS, AND PRESENCE MATTER.

MY HEART FINALLY AGREED WITH MY MIND.

ACT ONE: IT TRIED TO DESTROY ME

MORNING THOUGHTS

Date: Mood:

I Woke Up Feeling: Today I Will Intentionally Focus On:

Did I Wake Up Today Feeling Better Than I Did Yesterday?   Today I Want God To Know:

Today I Am Affirming: I Know I Am Worthy Of:

What Do I Believe I Will Need Help With Today?   Today I Want To Release:

What Will I Do Today That Will Help Me To Feel Happy & Relaxed?   Today I Am Reclaiming:

ACT ONE: IT TRIED TO DESTROY ME

NIGHTLY THOUGHTS

How Do I Currently Feel And Why Do I Feel This Way?

Tomorrow I Look Forward To:

Today's Breakup Symptoms:

Did My Ex Try To Get My Attention In Any Way Today?

Today I Learned:

If I Responded Yes To The Previous Prompt, Explain How:

Today I Was Tempted To:

Did I Do A Good Job Today Of Protecting My Peace And Space?

Did I Act On The Thing I Was Tempted To Do? If So, Why Did I Give In To It, And What Were The Results Of My Actions?

What Could I Have Done A Better Job With Today?

What Did I Tell My Ex Today, And If I Didn't Speak To Them, What Would I Want To Tell My Ex?

Tatiana's Personal Note: To Someone Who Loves You, You Are Everything They Hoped For.

ACT ONE: IT TRIED TO DESTROY ME

MORNING THOUGHTS

Date: Mood:

I Woke Up Feeling: Today I Will Intentionally Focus On:

Did I Wake Up Today Feeling Better Than I Did Yesterday?   Today I Want God To Know:

Today I Am Affirming: I Know I Am Worthy Of:

What Do I Believe I Will Need Help With Today?   Today I Want To Release:

What Will I Do Today That Will Help Me To Feel Happy & Relaxed?   Today I Am Reclaiming:

ACT ONE: IT TRIED TO DESTROY ME
NIGHTLY THOUGHTS

How Do I Currently Feel And Why Do I Feel This Way?

Did My Ex Try To Get My Attention In Any Way Today?

If I Responded Yes To The Previous Prompt, Explain How:

Did I Do A Good Job Today Of Protecting My Peace And Space?

What Could I Have Done A Better Job With Today?

Tomorrow I Look Forward To:

Today's Breakup Symptoms:

Today I Learned:

Today I Was Tempted To:

Did I Act On The Thing I Was Tempted To Do? If So, Why Did I Give In To It, And What Were The Results Of My Actions?

What Did I Tell My Ex Today, And If I Didn't Speak To Them, What Would I Want To Tell My Ex?

Tatiana's Personal Note: Every Morning, Intentionally Choose Positive Thoughts To Think About Yourself.

ACT ONE: IT TRIED TO DESTROY ME

MORNING THOUGHTS

Date: Mood:

I Woke Up Feeling: Today I Will Intentionally Focus On:

Did I Wake Up Today Feeling Better Than I Did Yesterday? Today I Want God To Know:

Today I Am Affirming: I Know I Am Worthy Of:

What Do I Believe I Will Need Help With Today?   Today I Want To Release:

What Will I Do Today That Will Help Me To Feel Happy & Relaxed?   Today I Am Reclaiming:

ACT ONE: IT TRIED TO DESTROY ME

NIGHTLY THOUGHTS

How Do I Currently Feel And Why Do I Feel This Way?

Tomorrow I Look Forward To:

Today's Breakup Symptoms:

Did My Ex Try To Get My Attention In Any Way Today?

Today I Learned:

If I Responded Yes To The Previous Prompt, Explain How:

Today I Was Tempted To:

Did I Do A Good Job Today Of Protecting My Peace And Space?

Did I Act On The Thing I Was Tempted To Do? If So, Why Did I Give In To It, And What Were The Results Of My Actions?

What Could I Have Done A Better Job With Today?

What Did I Tell My Ex Today, And If I Didn't Speak To Them, What Would I Want To Tell My Ex?

Tatiana's Personal Note: At Some Point, You Will Realize That YOU Need You.

ACT ONE: IT TRIED TO DESTROY ME

MORNING THOUGHTS

Date: Mood:

I Woke Up Feeling: | Today I Will Intentionally Focus On:

Did I Wake Up Today Feeling Better Than I Did Yesterday? | Today I Want God To Know:

Today I Am Affirming: | I Know I Am Worthy Of:

What Do I Believe I Will Need Help With Today? | Today I Want To Release:

What Will I Do Today That Will Help Me To Feel Happy & Relaxed? | Today I Am Reclaiming:

ACT ONE: IT TRIED TO DESTROY ME

NIGHTLY THOUGHTS

How Do I Currently Feel And Why Do I Feel This Way?

Tomorrow I Look Forward To:

Today's Breakup Symptoms:

Did My Ex Try To Get My Attention In Any Way Today?

Today I Learned:

If I Responded Yes To The Previous Prompt, Explain How:

Today I Was Tempted To:

Did I Do A Good Job Today Of Protecting My Peace And Space?

Did I Act On The Thing I Was Tempted To Do? If So, Why Did I Give In To It, And What Were The Results Of My Actions?

What Could I Have Done A Better Job With Today?

What Did I Tell My Ex Today, And If I Didn't Speak To Them, What Would I Want To Tell My Ex?

Tatiana's Personal Note: Sometimes You Do Not Need Closure. Sometimes You Just Need To Move On.

ACT ONE: IT TRIED TO DESTROY ME
MORNING THOUGHTS

Date: Mood:

I Woke Up Feeling: Today I Will Intentionally Focus On:

Did I Wake Up Today Feeling Better Than I Did   Today I Want God To Know:
Yesterday?

Today I Am Affirming: I Know I Am Worthy Of:

What Do I Believe I Will Need Help With   Today I Want To Release:
Today?

What Will I Do Today That Will Help Me To   Today I Am Reclaiming:
Feel Happy & Relaxed?

ACT ONE: IT TRIED TO DESTROY ME

NIGHTLY THOUGHTS

How Do I Currently Feel And Why Do I Feel This Way?

Tomorrow I Look Forward To:

Today's Breakup Symptoms:

Did My Ex Try To Get My Attention In Any Way Today?

Today I Learned:

If I Responded Yes To The Previous Prompt, Explain How:

Today I Was Tempted To:

Did I Do A Good Job Today Of Protecting My Peace And Space?

Did I Act On The Thing I Was Tempted To Do? If So, Why Did I Give In To It, And What Were The Results Of My Actions?

What Could I Have Done A Better Job With Today?

What Did I Tell My Ex Today, And If I Didn't Speak To Them, What Would I Want To Tell My Ex?

Tatiana's Personal Note: Some Things Are Temporary, But The Love You Have For Yourself Should Be Forever.

ACT ONE: IT TRIED TO DESTROY ME

MORNING THOUGHTS

Date: Mood:

I Woke Up Feeling: Today I Will Intentionally Focus On:

Did I Wake Up Today Feeling Better Than I Did Yesterday?   Today I Want God To Know:

Today I Am Affirming: I Know I Am Worthy Of:

What Do I Believe I Will Need Help With Today?   Today I Want To Release:

What Will I Do Today That Will Help Me To Feel Happy & Relaxed?   Today I Am Reclaiming:

ACT ONE: IT TRIED TO DESTROY ME

NIGHTLY THOUGHTS

How Do I Currently Feel And Why Do I Feel This Way?

Did My Ex Try To Get My Attention In Any Way Today?

If I Responded Yes To The Previous Prompt, Explain How:

Did I Do A Good Job Today Of Protecting My Peace And Space?

What Could I Have Done A Better Job With Today?

Tomorrow I Look Forward To:

Today's Breakup Symptoms:

Today I Learned:

Today I Was Tempted To:

Did I Act On The Thing I Was Tempted To Do? If So, Why Did I Give In To It, And What Were The Results Of My Actions?

What Did I Tell My Ex Today, And If I Didn't Speak To Them, What Would I Want To Tell My Ex?

Tatiana's Personal Note: It Does Not Matter What They See. The Only Thing That Matters Is How You See Yourself.

I WANT WHAT GOD WANTS FOR ME.

OWN WHO YOU ARE.

ENTERING MY LOVE (HER) GIRL ERA.

ACT TWO:
NOW I AM BACK

ABOUT THIS SECTION

Welcome to the section dedicated solely to your personal journey. Here, you will embark on a profound exploration of what it truly means to prioritize your needs. You will reflect on what you are ready to release, while simultaneously cultivating a deep understanding of the habits and thoughts you wish to adopt to fortify your strength. This is the moment to evaluate your evolving identity and discern whether you truly comprehend who you are becoming.

You will come to understand that the words of others hold no power over you unless you grant it. At this juncture, your self-perception and your inner dialogue are of paramount importance. You will learn to nurture yourself from within, valuing your thoughts, your tranquility, and your time as essential components of your well-being.

I encourage you to engage with the following questions during your morning routine. This practice will not only set a positive tone for your day but will also keep your personal goals in sharp focus.

Let us begin this transformative journey.

ACT TWO: NOW I AM BACK
MORNING THOUGHTS

Date: Mood:

Today, I Am Defining Myself As: What Qualities From My Past
                                                     Relationship Have I Found In Myself?

Today, I Am Affirming: I Want God To Know:

I Woke Up Visualizing: Today, I Plan To:

Today, I Desire: I Realize That I Have The Power To:

Yesterday, I Regained: What New Experience Do I Intend To
                                                     Embrace Today?

Tatiana's Personal Note: I Use My Pain To Empower Me, Not Control Me.
I Turned My Pain Into My Motivation.

ACT TWO: NOW I AM BACK
MORNING THOUGHTS

Date: Mood:

Today, I Am Defining Myself As: What Qualities From My Past Relationship Have I Found In Myself?

Today, I Am Affirming: I Want God To Know:

I Woke Up Visualizing: Today, I Plan To:

Today, I Desire: I Realize That I Have The Power To:

Yesterday, I Regained: What New Experience Do I Intend To Embrace Today?

Tatiana's Personal Note: When Someone Tells You That You Are Beautiful, Believe Them. That Is God Admiring His Work.

ACT TWO: NOW I AM BACK
MORNING THOUGHTS

Date: Mood:

Today, I Am Defining Myself As: What Qualities From My Past
                                                   Relationship Have I Found In Myself?

Today, I Am Affirming: I Want God To Know:

I Woke Up Visualizing: Today, I Plan To:

Today, I Desire: I Realize That I Have The Power To:

Yesterday, I Regained: What New Experience Do I Intend To
                                                   Embrace Today?

Tatiana's Personal Note: A Great Life Is Built On Loving God, Yourself, And Others.

ACT TWO: NOW I AM BACK
MORNING THOUGHTS

Date: Mood:

Today, I Am Defining Myself As: What Qualities From My Past
                                                   Relationship Have I Found In Myself?

Today, I Am Affirming: I Want God To Know:

I Woke Up Visualizing: Today, I Plan To:

Today, I Desire: I Realize That I Have The Power To:

Yesterday, I Regained: What New Experience Do I Intend To
                                                   Embrace Today?

Tatiana's Personal Note: Learn To Live In Peace.

ACT TWO: NOW I AM BACK
MORNING THOUGHTS

Date: Mood:

Today, I Am Defining Myself As: What Qualities From My Past
                                         Relationship Have I Found In Myself?

Today, I Am Affirming: I Want God To Know:

I Woke Up Visualizing: Today, I Plan To:

Today, I Desire: I Realize That I Have The Power To:

Yesterday, I Regained: What New Experience Do I Intend To
                                         Embrace Today?

Tatiana's Personal Note: First, Be A Great Friend To Yourself.

ACT TWO: NOW I AM BACK
MORNING THOUGHTS

Date: Mood:

Today, I Am Defining Myself As: What Qualities From My Past Relationship Have I Found In Myself?

Today, I Am Affirming: I Want God To Know:

I Woke Up Visualizing: Today, I Plan To:

Today, I Desire: I Realize That I Have The Power To:

Yesterday, I Regained: What New Experience Do I Intend To Embrace Today?

Tatiana's Personal Note: Take Care Of Your Soul.

ACT TWO: NOW I AM BACK
MORNING THOUGHTS

Date: Mood:

Today, I Am Defining Myself As: | What Qualities From My Past Relationship Have I Found In Myself?

Today, I Am Affirming: | I Want God To Know:

I Woke Up Visualizing: | Today, I Plan To:

Today, I Desire: | I Realize That I Have The Power To:

Yesterday, I Regained: | What New Experience Do I Intend To Embrace Today?

Tatiana's Personal Note: They Will Always Wonder How You Keep Winning.

**ALL I HAVE TO SAY
IS NEVER AGAIN.**

I HELD ON FOR A VERY LONG TIME, BUT NOW I FINALLY DECIDED TO LET GO.

ACT TWO: NOW I AM BACK
MORNING THOUGHTS

Date: Mood:

Today, I Am Defining Myself As: What Qualities From My Past Relationship Have I Found In Myself?

Today, I Am Affirming: I Want God To Know:

I Woke Up Visualizing: Today, I Plan To:

Today, I Desire: I Realize That I Have The Power To:

Yesterday, I Regained: What New Experience Do I Intend To Embrace Today?

Tatiana's Personal Note: Good Hearts Do Exist.

ACT TWO: NOW I AM BACK
MORNING THOUGHTS

Date: Mood:

Today, I Am Defining Myself As: What Qualities From My Past
                                               Relationship Have I Found In Myself?

Today, I Am Affirming: I Want God To Know:

I Woke Up Visualizing: Today, I Plan To:

Today, I Desire: I Realize That I Have The Power To:

Yesterday, I Regained: What New Experience Do I Intend To
                                               Embrace Today?

Tatiana's Personal Note: Grow And Fall In Love.

ACT TWO: NOW I AM BACK
MORNING THOUGHTS

Date: Mood:

Today, I Am Defining Myself As: What Qualities From My Past
                                                Relationship Have I Found In Myself?

Today, I Am Affirming: I Want God To Know:

I Woke Up Visualizing: Today, I Plan To:

Today, I Desire: I Realize That I Have The Power To:

Yesterday, I Regained: What New Experience Do I Intend To
                                                Embrace Today?

Tatiana's Personal Note: You Are What Someone Is Dreaming About.

ACT TWO: NOW I AM BACK
MORNING THOUGHTS

Date: Mood:

Today, I Am Defining Myself As: What Qualities From My Past
                                             Relationship Have I Found In Myself?

Today, I Am Affirming: I Want God To Know:

I Woke Up Visualizing: Today, I Plan To:

Today, I Desire: I Realize That I Have The Power To:

Yesterday, I Regained: What New Experience Do I Intend To
                                             Embrace Today?

Tatiana's Personal Note: Always Be The First To Choose You.

MY SELF-RESPECT IS NOW STRONGER THAN MY FEELINGS.

I CAN NOW LAUGH AT WHAT I THOUGHT I WANTED.

ACT TWO: NOW I AM BACK
MORNING THOUGHTS

Date: Mood:

Today, I Am Defining Myself As: What Qualities From My Past
                                                        Relationship Have I Found In Myself?

Today, I Am Affirming: I Want God To Know:

I Woke Up Visualizing: Today, I Plan To:

Today, I Desire: I Realize That I Have The Power To:

Yesterday, I Regained: What New Experience Do I Intend To
                                                        Embrace Today?

Tatiana's Personal Note: Always Remember You Were Built For Greatness.

ACT TWO: NOW I AM BACK
MORNING THOUGHTS

Date: Mood:

Today, I Am Defining Myself As: What Qualities From My Past Relationship Have I Found In Myself?

Today, I Am Affirming: I Want God To Know:

I Woke Up Visualizing: Today, I Plan To:

Today, I Desire: I Realize That I Have The Power To:

Yesterday, I Regained: What New Experience Do I Intend To Embrace Today?

Tatiana's Personal Note: What Was Supposed To Harm You, Embarrass You, Destroy You, And Play You Didn't Know It Was Simply A Blessing In Disguise.

ACT TWO: NOW I AM BACK
MORNING THOUGHTS

Date: Mood:

Today, I Am Defining Myself As: What Qualities From My Past
                                         Relationship Have I Found In Myself?

Today, I Am Affirming: I Want God To Know:

I Woke Up Visualizing: Today, I Plan To:

Today, I Desire: I Realize That I Have The Power To:

Yesterday, I Regained: What New Experience Do I Intend To
                                         Embrace Today?

Tatiana's Personal Note: It Is Not Easy, But It Gets Better.

ACT TWO: NOW I AM BACK
MORNING THOUGHTS

Date: Mood:

Today, I Am Defining Myself As: What Qualities From My Past
                                                         Relationship Have I Found In Myself?

Today, I Am Affirming: I Want God To Know:

I Woke Up Visualizing: Today, I Plan To:

Today, I Desire: I Realize That I Have The Power To:

Yesterday, I Regained: What New Experience Do I Intend To
                                                         Embrace Today?

**Tatiana's Personal Note: Allow What Wants To Go, To Go,
So You Can Make Space For What Needs To Come.**

YOU DON'T NEED ANYONE'S VALIDATION. YOU'VE GOT THIS.

AS SOON AS I STARTED HEALING THE PARTS OF ME THAT WERE HURT, I STOPPED ATTRACTING BROKEN PEOPLE.

ACT TWO: NOW I AM BACK
MORNING THOUGHTS

Date: Mood:

Today, I Am Defining Myself As: What Qualities From My Past
                                         Relationship Have I Found In Myself?

Today, I Am Affirming: I Want God To Know:

I Woke Up Visualizing: Today, I Plan To:

Today, I Desire: I Realize That I Have The Power To:

Yesterday, I Regained: What New Experience Do I Intend To
                                         Embrace Today?

Tatiana's Personal Note: They May Have Been With You,
But They Were Never For You.

ACT TWO: NOW I AM BACK
MORNING THOUGHTS

Date: Mood:

Today, I Am Defining Myself As: What Qualities From My Past
                                                  Relationship Have I Found In Myself?

Today, I Am Affirming: I Want God To Know:

I Woke Up Visualizing: Today, I Plan To:

Today, I Desire: I Realize That I Have The Power To:

Yesterday, I Regained: What New Experience Do I Intend To
                                                  Embrace Today?

Tatiana's Personal Note: You Should Never Have To Beg For Something You Can Give Yourself.

ACT TWO: NOW I AM BACK
MORNING THOUGHTS

Date: Mood:

Today, I Am Defining Myself As: What Qualities From My Past Relationship Have I Found In Myself?

Today, I Am Affirming: I Want God To Know:

I Woke Up Visualizing: Today, I Plan To:

Today, I Desire: I Realize That I Have The Power To:

Yesterday, I Regained: What New Experience Do I Intend To Embrace Today?

Tatiana's Personal Note: There Is Nothing Wrong With Over-Loving Yourself.

ACT TWO: NOW I AM BACK
MORNING THOUGHTS

Date: Mood:

Today, I Am Defining Myself As: What Qualities From My Past
                                                   Relationship Have I Found In Myself?

Today, I Am Affirming: I Want God To Know:

I Woke Up Visualizing: Today, I Plan To:

Today, I Desire: I Realize That I Have The Power To:

Yesterday, I Regained: What New Experience Do I Intend To
                                                   Embrace Today?

Tatiana's Personal Note: Being Whole All On Your Own .... That Is More Than Enough.

ACT TWO: NOW I AM BACK
MORNING THOUGHTS

Date: Mood:

Today, I Am Defining Myself As: What Qualities From My Past
                                                        Relationship Have I Found In Myself?

Today, I Am Affirming: I Want God To Know:

I Woke Up Visualizing: Today, I Plan To:

Today, I Desire: I Realize That I Have The Power To:

Yesterday, I Regained: What New Experience Do I Intend To
                                                        Embrace Today?

Tatiana's Personal Note: Never Be Afraid To Shine.

ACT TWO: NOW I AM BACK
MORNING THOUGHTS

Date: Mood:

Today, I Am Defining Myself As: What Qualities From My Past
                                                   Relationship Have I Found In Myself?

Today, I Am Affirming: I Want God To Know:

I Woke Up Visualizing: Today, I Plan To:

Today, I Desire: I Realize That I Have The Power To:

Yesterday, I Regained: What New Experience Do I Intend To
                                                   Embrace Today?

Tatiana's Personal Note: Be In The Business Of Investing In Yourself.

ACT TWO: NOW I AM BACK
MORNING THOUGHTS

Date: Mood:

Today, I Am Defining Myself As: What Qualities From My Past Relationship Have I Found In Myself?

Today, I Am Affirming: I Want God To Know:

I Woke Up Visualizing: Today, I Plan To:

Today, I Desire: I Realize That I Have The Power To:

Yesterday, I Regained: What New Experience Do I Intend To Embrace Today?

Tatiana's Personal Note: It Is Time To Level Up.

LOVE ALWAYS RETURNS.
IT MAY COME IN THE FORM OF
A NEW PERSON, ENVIRONMENT,
OR ROUTINE, BUT LOVE ALWAYS
COMES BACK.

WRITE YOURSELF VOWS NO ONE ELSE CAN BREAK.

ACT TWO: NOW I AM BACK
MORNING THOUGHTS

Date: Mood:

Today, I Am Defining Myself As: What Qualities From My Past Relationship Have I Found In Myself?

Today, I Am Affirming: I Want God To Know:

I Woke Up Visualizing: Today, I Plan To:

Today, I Desire: I Realize That I Have The Power To:

Yesterday, I Regained: What New Experience Do I Intend To Embrace Today?

Tatiana's Personal Note: Release. Replenish. Revamp.

ACT TWO: NOW I AM BACK
MORNING THOUGHTS

Date:	Mood:
Today, I Am Defining Myself As:	What Qualities From My Past Relationship Have I Found In Myself?
Today, I Am Affirming:	I Want God To Know:
I Woke Up Visualizing:	Today, I Plan To:
Today, I Desire:	I Realize That I Have The Power To:
Yesterday, I Regained:	What New Experience Do I Intend To Embrace Today?

Tatiana's Personal Note: Always Stay Grateful.

ACT TWO: NOW I AM BACK
MORNING THOUGHTS

Date: Mood:

Today, I Am Defining Myself As: What Qualities From My Past
                                                Relationship Have I Found In Myself?

Today, I Am Affirming: I Want God To Know:

I Woke Up Visualizing: Today, I Plan To:

Today, I Desire: I Realize That I Have The Power To:

Yesterday, I Regained: What New Experience Do I Intend To
                                                Embrace Today?

Tatiana's Personal Note: You Do Not Need Anyone's Permission To Shine.

ACT TWO: NOW I AM BACK
MORNING THOUGHTS

Date: Mood:

Today, I Am Defining Myself As: What Qualities From My Past
                                                Relationship Have I Found In Myself?

Today, I Am Affirming: I Want God To Know:

I Woke Up Visualizing: Today, I Plan To:

Today, I Desire: I Realize That I Have The Power To:

Yesterday, I Regained: What New Experience Do I Intend To
                                                Embrace Today?

Tatiana's Personal Note: All Of YOU Needs You.

ACT TWO: NOW I AM BACK
MORNING THOUGHTS

Date: Mood:

Today, I Am Defining Myself As: What Qualities From My Past
                                                Relationship Have I Found In Myself?

Today, I Am Affirming: I Want God To Know:

I Woke Up Visualizing: Today, I Plan To:

Today, I Desire: I Realize That I Have The Power To:

Yesterday, I Regained: What New Experience Do I Intend To
                                                Embrace Today?

Tatiana's Personal Note: This Is The Beginning Of Loving Yourself All Over Again. Welcome Home.

SOME YEARS ARE FOR GROWING, BUT THIS YEAR IS FOR BLOOMING.

I BELONG TO ME BEFORE I BELONG TO ANYONE ELSE.

ACT TWO: NOW I AM BACK
MORNING THOUGHTS

Date: Mood:

Today, I Am Defining Myself As: What Qualities From My Past Relationship Have I Found In Myself?

Today, I Am Affirming: I Want God To Know:

I Woke Up Visualizing: Today, I Plan To:

Today, I Desire: I Realize That I Have The Power To:

Yesterday, I Regained: What New Experience Do I Intend To Embrace Today?

Tatiana's Personal Note: Trust In God's Process.

ACT TWO: NOW I AM BACK
MORNING THOUGHTS

Date: Mood:

Today, I Am Defining Myself As: What Qualities From My Past
                                               Relationship Have I Found In Myself?

Today, I Am Affirming: I Want God To Know:

I Woke Up Visualizing: Today, I Plan To:

Today, I Desire: I Realize That I Have The Power To:

Yesterday, I Regained: What New Experience Do I Intend To
                                               Embrace Today?

Tatiana's Personal Note: Learn To Nurture You.

ACT TWO: NOW I AM BACK
MORNING THOUGHTS

Date: Mood:

Today, I Am Defining Myself As: What Qualities From My Past
                                                  Relationship Have I Found In Myself?

Today, I Am Affirming: I Want God To Know:

I Woke Up Visualizing: Today, I Plan To:

Today, I Desire: I Realize That I Have The Power To:

Yesterday, I Regained: What New Experience Do I Intend To
                                                  Embrace Today?

Tatiana's Personal Note: It Is Okay If Your Happiness Is Obnoxious To Others - Let Go Of The Others.

ACT TWO: NOW I AM BACK
MORNING THOUGHTS

Date: Mood:

Today, I Am Defining Myself As: What Qualities From My Past
                                                   Relationship Have I Found In Myself?

Today, I Am Affirming: I Want God To Know:

I Woke Up Visualizing: Today, I Plan To:

Today, I Desire: I Realize That I Have The Power To:

Yesterday, I Regained: What New Experience Do I Intend To
                                                   Embrace Today?

Tatiana's Personal Note: God Has Answered Your Prayer.

ACT TWO: NOW I AM BACK
MORNING THOUGHTS

Date: Mood:

Today, I Am Defining Myself As: What Qualities From My Past Relationship Have I Found In Myself?

Today, I Am Affirming: I Want God To Know:

I Woke Up Visualizing: Today, I Plan To:

Today, I Desire: I Realize That I Have The Power To:

Yesterday, I Regained: What New Experience Do I Intend To Embrace Today?

Tatiana's Personal Note: Be Prepared For Joy.

ACT TWO: NOW I AM BACK
MORNING THOUGHTS

Date: Mood:

Today, I Am Defining Myself As: What Qualities From My Past
                                                Relationship Have I Found In Myself?

Today, I Am Affirming: I Want God To Know:

I Woke Up Visualizing: Today, I Plan To:

Today, I Desire: I Realize That I Have The Power To:

Yesterday, I Regained: What New Experience Do I Intend To
                                                Embrace Today?

Tatiana's Personal Note: Show Up For Yourself.

ACT TWO: NOW I AM BACK
MORNING THOUGHTS

Date: Mood:

Today, I Am Defining Myself As: What Qualities From My Past Relationship Have I Found In Myself?

Today, I Am Affirming: I Want God To Know:

I Woke Up Visualizing: Today, I Plan To:

Today, I Desire: I Realize That I Have The Power To:

Yesterday, I Regained: What New Experience Do I Intend To Embrace Today?

Tatiana's Personal Note: Prove Yourself To Yourself.

IT FEELS GOOD TO BE REMOVED FROM THE CHAOS.

SOME THINGS HAVE TO END FOR BETTER THINGS TO BEGIN.

ACT TWO: NOW I AM BACK
MORNING THOUGHTS

Date: Mood:

Today, I Am Defining Myself As: What Qualities From My Past
                                                   Relationship Have I Found In Myself?

Today, I Am Affirming: I Want God To Know:

I Woke Up Visualizing: Today, I Plan To:

Today, I Desire: I Realize That I Have The Power To:

Yesterday, I Regained: What New Experience Do I Intend To
                                                   Embrace Today?

Tatiana's Personal Note: Forgiveness Is Love. Show Love To Yourself.

ACT TWO: NOW I AM BACK
MORNING THOUGHTS

Date: Mood:

Today, I Am Defining Myself As: What Qualities From My Past Relationship Have I Found In Myself?

Today, I Am Affirming: I Want God To Know:

I Woke Up Visualizing: Today, I Plan To:

Today, I Desire: I Realize That I Have The Power To:

Yesterday, I Regained: What New Experience Do I Intend To Embrace Today?

Tatiana's Personal Note: They Will Never Be Able To Tell Your Story Like You Can. That's Okay.

ACT TWO: NOW I AM BACK
MORNING THOUGHTS

Date: Mood:

Today, I Am Defining Myself As: What Qualities From My Past
                                        Relationship Have I Found In Myself?

Today, I Am Affirming: I Want God To Know:

I Woke Up Visualizing: Today, I Plan To:

Today, I Desire: I Realize That I Have The Power To:

Yesterday, I Regained: What New Experience Do I Intend To
                                        Embrace Today?

Tatiana's Personal Note: Your Morals Should Be Non-Negotiable.

ACT TWO: NOW I AM BACK
MORNING THOUGHTS

Date: Mood:

Today, I Am Defining Myself As: What Qualities From My Past
                                                         Relationship Have I Found In Myself?

Today, I Am Affirming: I Want God To Know:

I Woke Up Visualizing: Today, I Plan To:

Today, I Desire: I Realize That I Have The Power To:

Yesterday, I Regained: What New Experience Do I Intend To
                                                         Embrace Today?

Tatiana's Personal Note: Another Person's Opinion Of You Should Never Truly Matter.

ACT TWO: NOW I AM BACK
MORNING THOUGHTS

Date: Mood:

Today, I Am Defining Myself As: What Qualities From My Past Relationship Have I Found In Myself?

Today, I Am Affirming: I Want God To Know:

I Woke Up Visualizing: Today, I Plan To:

Today, I Desire: I Realize That I Have The Power To:

Yesterday, I Regained: What New Experience Do I Intend To Embrace Today?

Tatiana's Personal Note: Some Great Things Are Happening To You Right Now.

ACT TWO: NOW I AM BACK
MORNING THOUGHTS

Date: Mood:

Today, I Am Defining Myself As: What Qualities From My Past
                                               Relationship Have I Found In Myself?

Today, I Am Affirming: I Want God To Know:

I Woke Up Visualizing: Today, I Plan To:

Today, I Desire: I Realize That I Have The Power To:

Yesterday, I Regained: What New Experience Do I Intend To
                                               Embrace Today?

==Tatiana's Personal Note: It Is Okay To Start Over With A New Set Of Standards.==

ACT TWO: NOW I AM BACK
MORNING THOUGHTS

Date: Mood:

Today, I Am Defining Myself As: What Qualities From My Past Relationship Have I Found In Myself?

Today, I Am Affirming: I Want God To Know:

I Woke Up Visualizing: Today, I Plan To:

Today, I Desire: I Realize That I Have The Power To:

Yesterday, I Regained: What New Experience Do I Intend To Embrace Today?

Tatiana's Personal Note: Remember, You Are Not What They Are Used To.

THE MINDSET MATTERS.

MY VOICE MATTERS.

ACT TWO: NOW I AM BACK
MORNING THOUGHTS

Date: Mood:

Today, I Am Defining Myself As: What Qualities From My Past Relationship Have I Found In Myself?

Today, I Am Affirming: I Want God To Know:

I Woke Up Visualizing: Today, I Plan To:

Today, I Desire: I Realize That I Have The Power To:

Yesterday, I Regained: What New Experience Do I Intend To Embrace Today?

Tatiana's Personal Note: Sometimes, They Think If You Lose Them, You've Lost In Life. They Don't Realize That You've Actually Won.

ACT TWO: NOW I AM BACK
MORNING THOUGHTS

Date:

Mood:

Today, I Am Defining Myself As:

What Qualities From My Past Relationship Have I Found In Myself?

Today, I Am Affirming:

I Want God To Know:

I Woke Up Visualizing:

Today, I Plan To:

Today, I Desire:

I Realize That I Have The Power To:

Yesterday, I Regained:

What New Experience Do I Intend To Embrace Today?

Tatiana's Personal Note: You Need YOU To Love You.

ACT TWO: NOW I AM BACK
MORNING THOUGHTS

Date: Mood:

Today, I Am Defining Myself As: What Qualities From My Past Relationship Have I Found In Myself?

Today, I Am Affirming: I Want God To Know:

I Woke Up Visualizing: Today, I Plan To:

Today, I Desire: I Realize That I Have The Power To:

Yesterday, I Regained: What New Experience Do I Intend To Embrace Today?

Tatiana's Personal Note: The Old Way Will Never Measure Up To Your New Mindset.

PEACE OF MIND.
I HAVE THAT NOW.

LIFE IS LOVING
ME RIGHT BACK.

ACT TWO: NOW I AM BACK
MORNING THOUGHTS

Date: Mood:

Today, I Am Defining Myself As: What Qualities From My Past
                                                  Relationship Have I Found In Myself?

Today, I Am Affirming: I Want God To Know:

I Woke Up Visualizing: Today, I Plan To:

Today, I Desire: I Realize That I Have The Power To:

Yesterday, I Regained: What New Experience Do I Intend To
                                                  Embrace Today?

Tatiana's Personal Note: You Are Worthy Of True Love.

ACT TWO: NOW I AM BACK
MORNING THOUGHTS

Date: Mood:

Today, I Am Defining Myself As: What Qualities From My Past Relationship Have I Found In Myself?

Today, I Am Affirming: I Want God To Know:

I Woke Up Visualizing: Today, I Plan To:

Today, I Desire: I Realize That I Have The Power To:

Yesterday, I Regained: What New Experience Do I Intend To Embrace Today?

Tatiana's Personal Note: No More Thinking Small Towards The Things You Want In Life.

ACT TWO: NOW I AM BACK
MORNING THOUGHTS

Date: Mood:

Today, I Am Defining Myself As: What Qualities From My Past
                                                   Relationship Have I Found In Myself?

Today, I Am Affirming: I Want God To Know:

I Woke Up Visualizing: Today, I Plan To:

Today, I Desire: I Realize That I Have The Power To:

Yesterday, I Regained: What New Experience Do I Intend To
                                                   Embrace Today?

Tatiana's Personal Note: Your Future Does Not Have To Look Like Your Past.

ACT TWO: NOW I AM BACK
MORNING THOUGHTS

Date: Mood:

Today, I Am Defining Myself As: What Qualities From My Past
                                                Relationship Have I Found In Myself?

Today, I Am Affirming: I Want God To Know:

I Woke Up Visualizing: Today, I Plan To:

Today, I Desire: I Realize That I Have The Power To:

Yesterday, I Regained: What New Experience Do I Intend To
                                                Embrace Today?

==Tatiana's Personal Note: Declare Your Greatness Today.==

ACT TWO: NOW I AM BACK
MORNING THOUGHTS

Date:

Mood:

Today, I Am Defining Myself As:

What Qualities From My Past Relationship Have I Found In Myself?

Today, I Am Affirming:

I Want God To Know:

I Woke Up Visualizing:

Today, I Plan To:

Today, I Desire:

I Realize That I Have The Power To:

Yesterday, I Regained:

What New Experience Do I Intend To Embrace Today?

Tatiana's Personal Note: Your Faith Is Your Biggest Blessing.

ACT TWO: NOW I AM BACK
MORNING THOUGHTS

Date: Mood:

Today, I Am Defining Myself As: What Qualities From My Past
                                                Relationship Have I Found In Myself?

Today, I Am Affirming: I Want God To Know:

I Woke Up Visualizing: Today, I Plan To:

Today, I Desire: I Realize That I Have The Power To:

Yesterday, I Regained: What New Experience Do I Intend To
                                                Embrace Today?

Tatiana's Personal Note: You Are More Than Your Mistakes.

ACT TWO: NOW I AM BACK
MORNING THOUGHTS

Date: Mood:

Today, I Am Defining Myself As: What Qualities From My Past
                                                         Relationship Have I Found In Myself?

Today, I Am Affirming: I Want God To Know:

I Woke Up Visualizing: Today, I Plan To:

Today, I Desire: I Realize That I Have The Power To:

Yesterday, I Regained: What New Experience Do I Intend To
                                                         Embrace Today?

Tatiana's Personal Note: There Is Greatness Within You.

I WILL ALWAYS BE THE FIRST TO CHOOSE ME.

I WANT YOU TO FEEL EVERY BIT OF ME - EVEN THE PARTS THAT HURT. MAYBE THEN YOU'LL UNDERSTAND.

ACT TWO: NOW I AM BACK
MORNING THOUGHTS

Date: Mood:

Today, I Am Defining Myself As: | What Qualities From My Past Relationship Have I Found In Myself?

Today, I Am Affirming: | I Want God To Know:

I Woke Up Visualizing: | Today, I Plan To:

Today, I Desire: | I Realize That I Have The Power To:

Yesterday, I Regained: | What New Experience Do I Intend To Embrace Today?

Tatiana's Personal Note: You Can Choose To Move On To The Next Level Of You At Any Time.

ACT TWO: NOW I AM BACK
MORNING THOUGHTS

Date: Mood:

Today, I Am Defining Myself As: What Qualities From My Past
                                                  Relationship Have I Found In Myself?

Today, I Am Affirming: I Want God To Know:

I Woke Up Visualizing: Today, I Plan To:

Today, I Desire: I Realize That I Have The Power To:

Yesterday, I Regained: What New Experience Do I Intend To
                                                  Embrace Today?

Tatiana's Personal Note: Promise Yourself To Always Connect With Good Energy.

ACT TWO: NOW I AM BACK
MORNING THOUGHTS

Date: Mood:

Today, I Am Defining Myself As: What Qualities From My Past Relationship Have I Found In Myself?

Today, I Am Affirming: I Want God To Know:

I Woke Up Visualizing: Today, I Plan To:

Today, I Desire: I Realize That I Have The Power To:

Yesterday, I Regained: What New Experience Do I Intend To Embrace Today?

Tatiana's Personal Note: Give Yourself The Love You Easily Give To Others.

ACT TWO: NOW I AM BACK
MORNING THOUGHTS

Date: Mood:

Today, I Am Defining Myself As: What Qualities From My Past
                                                Relationship Have I Found In Myself?

Today, I Am Affirming: I Want God To Know:

I Woke Up Visualizing: Today, I Plan To:

Today, I Desire: I Realize That I Have The Power To:

Yesterday, I Regained: What New Experience Do I Intend To
                                                Embrace Today?

Tatiana's Personal Note: You Do Not Have To Ride The Wave
When You Are The Wave.

I DESERVE MORE
THAN A SORRY.

I TOLD MYSELF....
I GOT YOU.

ACT TWO: NOW I AM BACK
MORNING THOUGHTS

Date: Mood:

Today, I Am Defining Myself As: What Qualities From My Past Relationship Have I Found In Myself?

Today, I Am Affirming: I Want God To Know:

I Woke Up Visualizing: Today, I Plan To:

Today, I Desire: I Realize That I Have The Power To:

Yesterday, I Regained: What New Experience Do I Intend To Embrace Today?

Tatiana's Personal Note: It's Time To Get Your Confidence At A Full Tank.

ACT TWO: NOW I AM BACK
MORNING THOUGHTS

Date: Mood:

Today, I Am Defining Myself As: What Qualities From My Past
                                                  Relationship Have I Found In Myself?

Today, I Am Affirming: I Want God To Know:

I Woke Up Visualizing: Today, I Plan To:

Today, I Desire: I Realize That I Have The Power To:

Yesterday, I Regained: What New Experience Do I Intend To
                                                  Embrace Today?

Tatiana's Personal Note: That Someone Special In Your Life Is You.

ACT TWO: NOW I AM BACK
MORNING THOUGHTS

Date: Mood:

Today, I Am Defining Myself As: What Qualities From My Past Relationship Have I Found In Myself?

Today, I Am Affirming: I Want God To Know:

I Woke Up Visualizing: Today, I Plan To:

Today, I Desire: I Realize That I Have The Power To:

Yesterday, I Regained: What New Experience Do I Intend To Embrace Today?

Tatiana's Personal Note: No Longer Will The Fears Of Your Past Prevent You From Creating A Better Future.

ACT TWO: NOW I AM BACK
MORNING THOUGHTS

Date: Mood:

Today, I Am Defining Myself As: What Qualities From My Past
                                         Relationship Have I Found In Myself?

Today, I Am Affirming: I Want God To Know:

I Woke Up Visualizing: Today, I Plan To:

Today, I Desire: I Realize That I Have The Power To:

Yesterday, I Regained: What New Experience Do I Intend To
                                         Embrace Today?

Tatiana's Personal Note: Too Many People Settle. So Glad You Are Not One Of Them.

ACT TWO: NOW I AM BACK
MORNING THOUGHTS

Date: Mood:

Today, I Am Defining Myself As: What Qualities From My Past Relationship Have I Found In Myself?

Today, I Am Affirming: I Want God To Know:

I Woke Up Visualizing: Today, I Plan To:

Today, I Desire: I Realize That I Have The Power To:

Yesterday, I Regained: What New Experience Do I Intend To Embrace Today?

Tatiana's Personal Note: The Lord Is My Strength And My Defense; He Has Become My Salvation. – Psalms 118:14

ACT TWO: NOW I AM BACK
MORNING THOUGHTS

Date:

Mood:

Today, I Am Defining Myself As:

What Qualities From My Past Relationship Have I Found In Myself?

Today, I Am Affirming:

I Want God To Know:

I Woke Up Visualizing:

Today, I Plan To:

Today, I Desire:

I Realize That I Have The Power To:

Yesterday, I Regained:

What New Experience Do I Intend To Embrace Today?

Tatana's Personal Note: You Can Feel When The Love Is Real.

ACT THREE:
I AM NOT JUST ANYBODY

ABOUT THIS SECTION

Welcome to a realm of true liberation. You have gracefully moved beyond the past, and this space is devoted to cultivating the vision and expectation of the love you not only desire but are inherently worthy of. You may have once harbored doubts, dismissing the possibility of a new romantic chapter, but this section is designed to dissolve every barrier that stands between you and one of life's divine commandments—Love.

Why not step into the beauty of creation and trust in a new, breathtaking opportunity for love with a romantic partner? Whether you are currently in a relationship or seeking a fresh connection, you deserve a love life that is healthy, passionate, respectful, and mutually uplifting.

Before manifesting this profound love with another, you must first establish where you stand with yourself. What vows will you make to your soul? What truths do you want God to bear witness to? How will you recognize when you have found the one destined for you? Do you truly understand the depth of what you desire and need from your next relationship?

Begin your day by answering these reflective prompts and allow yourself the luxury of exploring your responses with intention. Resist the urge to hastily jot down fleeting thoughts—this is your sacred moment to articulate what you truly want. Trust that the love you envision is not only possible but already in your reach. If you find it difficult to believe in this future for yourself, dedicate extra care to cultivating that belief.

Let excitement fill your heart, and above all, enjoy the process. Watch as your desires elegantly unfold into reality, with every word you pen becoming a testament to the life and love you are calling forth.

ACT THREE: I AM NOT JUST ANYBODY

MORNING THOUGHTS

Date: Mood:

Today, I Affirm: My Future Relationship Will Feel:

I Feel Really Good About: Today, I Am Asking God:

I Know I Am: Today I Release _____
                                                                And Hope To Gain:

Today's Relationship With   I Am Excited About:
_____

Looks Like: Today, I Am Promising Myself:

My New Partner: I Am Choosing My Happiness Over:

Tatiana's Personal Note: Remember That What Tried To Hurt You Helped You.

ACT THREE: I AM NOT JUST ANYBODY
MORNING THOUGHTS

Date: Mood:

Today, I Affirm: My Future Relationship Will Feel:

I Feel Really Good About: Today, I Am Asking God:

I Know I Am: Today I Release _____
                                                         And Hope To Gain:

Today's Relationship With   I Am Excited About:

_____

Looks Like: Today, I Am Promising Myself:

My New Partner: I Am Choosing My Happiness Over:

Tatiana's Personal Note: Believe In The Best For Yourself.

ACT THREE: I AM NOT JUST ANYBODY
MORNING THOUGHTS

Date: Mood:

Today, I Affirm: My Future Relationship Will Feel:

I Feel Really Good About: Today, I Am Asking God:

I Know I Am: Today I Release _____
                                         And Hope To Gain:

Today's Relationship With   I Am Excited About:
_____

Looks Like: Today, I Am Promising Myself:

My New Partner: I Am Choosing My Happiness Over:

Tatiana's Personal Note: Believe In Yourself Before Anyone Else Can.

ACT THREE: I AM NOT JUST ANYBODY
MORNING THOUGHTS

Date: Mood:

Today, I Affirm: My Future Relationship Will Feel:

I Feel Really Good About: Today, I Am Asking God:

I Know I Am: Today I Release _____
                                         And Hope To Gain:

Today's Relationship With   I Am Excited About:
_____

Looks Like: Today, I Am Promising Myself:

My New Partner: I Am Choosing My Happiness Over:

Tatiana's Personal Note: Don't Be Afraid To Go After Everything You've Ever Wanted.

ACT THREE: I AM NOT JUST ANYBODY
MORNING THOUGHTS

Date: Mood:

Today, I Affirm: My Future Relationship Will Feel:

I Feel Really Good About: Today, I Am Asking God:

I Know I Am: Today I Release _____
                                                         And Hope To Gain:

Today's Relationship With   I Am Excited About:
_____

Looks Like: Today, I Am Promising Myself:

My New Partner: I Am Choosing My Happiness Over:

Tatiana's Personal Note: Do Not Let Your Fear Of Being Hurt Make You Miss The Chance To Be Happy.

ACT THREE: I AM NOT JUST ANYBODY
MORNING THOUGHTS

Date: Mood:

Today, I Affirm: My Future Relationship Will Feel:

I Feel Really Good About: Today, I Am Asking God:

I Know I Am: Today I Release _____
And Hope To Gain:

Today's Relationship With I Am Excited About:
_____

Looks Like: Today, I Am Promising Myself:

My New Partner: I Am Choosing My Happiness Over:

Tatiana's Personal Note: Upgrade Your Reality To Match Your Dreams.

ACT THREE: I AM NOT JUST ANYBODY
MORNING THOUGHTS

Date: Mood:

Today, I Affirm: My Future Relationship Will Feel:

I Feel Really Good About: Today, I Am Asking God:

I Know I Am: Today I Release _____
                                                              And Hope To Gain:

Today's Relationship With   I Am Excited About:

_____

Looks Like: Today, I Am Promising Myself:

My New Partner: I Am Choosing My Happiness Over:

Tatiana's Personal Note: If You Are Worth Pursuing, Stop Asking Why It's Taking Time.

I LOVE ME.

TRYING TO SEE MYSELF THE WAY GOD SEES ME. I CAUGHT A GLIMPSE OF THAT, AND MY CONFIDENCE IS ON ANOTHER LEVEL.

ACT THREE: I AM NOT JUST ANYBODY

MORNING THOUGHTS

Date: Mood:

Today, I Affirm: My Future Relationship Will Feel:

I Feel Really Good About: Today, I Am Asking God:

I Know I Am: Today I Release _____
                                                     And Hope To Gain:

Today's Relationship With   I Am Excited About:
_____

Looks Like: Today, I Am Promising Myself:

My New Partner: I Am Choosing My Happiness Over:

Tatiana's Personal Note: Be Okay With Taking A Chance On Love.

ACT THREE: I AM NOT JUST ANYBODY
MORNING THOUGHTS

Date: Mood:

Today, I Affirm: My Future Relationship Will Feel:

I Feel Really Good About: Today, I Am Asking God:

I Know I Am: Today I Release _____
                                                And Hope To Gain:

Today's Relationship With   I Am Excited About:

_____

Looks Like: Today, I Am Promising Myself:

My New Partner: I Am Choosing My Happiness Over:

Tatiana's Personal Note: Do Not Let The Fear Of The Unknown Keep You From What Belongs To You.

ACT THREE: I AM NOT JUST ANYBODY

MORNING THOUGHTS

Date: Mood:

Today, I Affirm: My Future Relationship Will Feel:

I Feel Really Good About: Today, I Am Asking God:

I Know I Am: Today I Release _____
                                                         And Hope To Gain:

Today's Relationship With   I Am Excited About:
_____

Looks Like: Today, I Am Promising Myself:

My New Partner: I Am Choosing My Happiness Over:

Tatiana's Personal Note: Love Is Calling.

ACT THREE: I AM NOT JUST ANYBODY
MORNING THOUGHTS

Date: Mood:

Today, I Affirm: My Future Relationship Will Feel:

I Feel Really Good About: Today, I Am Asking God:

I Know I Am: Today I Release _____
                                         And Hope To Gain:

Today's Relationship With   I Am Excited About:
_____

Looks Like: Today, I Am Promising Myself:

My New Partner: I Am Choosing My Happiness Over:

Tatiana's Personal Note: Be Mentally And Spiritually Available For Your Future.

ACT THREE: I AM NOT JUST ANYBODY
MORNING THOUGHTS

Date: Mood:

Today, I Affirm: My Future Relationship Will Feel:

I Feel Really Good About: Today, I Am Asking God:

I Know I Am: Today I Release _____
                                         And Hope To Gain:

Today's Relationship With   I Am Excited About:
_____

Looks Like: Today, I Am Promising Myself:

My New Partner: I Am Choosing My Happiness Over:

Tatiana's Personal Note: Your New Outlook Will Bring
In A New And Exciting Adventure.

ACT THREE: I AM NOT JUST ANYBODY
MORNING THOUGHTS

Date: Mood:

Today, I Affirm: My Future Relationship Will Feel:

I Feel Really Good About: Today, I Am Asking God:

I Know I Am: Today I Release _____
                                                           And Hope To Gain:

Today's Relationship With   I Am Excited About:
_____

Looks Like: Today, I Am Promising Myself:

My New Partner: I Am Choosing My Happiness Over:

Tatiana's Personal Note: Go Ahead. Make Your Request For New, Passionate, And Responsible Love.

ACT THREE: I AM NOT JUST ANYBODY

MORNING THOUGHTS

Date: Mood:

Today, I Affirm: My Future Relationship Will Feel:

I Feel Really Good About: Today, I Am Asking God:

I Know I Am: Today I Release _____
                                                 And Hope To Gain:

Today's Relationship With   I Am Excited About:
_____

Looks Like: Today, I Am Promising Myself:

My New Partner: I Am Choosing My Happiness Over:

Tatiana's Personal Note: Be Proud Of Who You Are.

I DO NOT JUST
LOOK LIKE LOVE.
I FEEL LIKE IT TOO.

MY ABILITY TO LOVE
AGAIN IS PHENOMENAL.

ACT THREE: I AM NOT JUST ANYBODY
MORNING THOUGHTS

Date: Mood:

Today, I Affirm: My Future Relationship Will Feel:

I Feel Really Good About: Today, I Am Asking God:

I Know I Am: Today I Release _____
                                                   And Hope To Gain:

Today's Relationship With   I Am Excited About:
_____

Looks Like: Today, I Am Promising Myself:

My New Partner: I Am Choosing My Happiness Over:

<mark>Tatiana's Personal Note: Be Hopeful About What And Who Is Coming Your Way.</mark>

ACT THREE: I AM NOT JUST ANYBODY
MORNING THOUGHTS

Date:

Mood:

Today, I Affirm:

My Future Relationship Will Feel:

I Feel Really Good About:

Today, I Am Asking God:

I Know I Am:

Today I Release _____
And Hope To Gain:

Today's Relationship With
_____

I Am Excited About:

Looks Like:

Today, I Am Promising Myself:

My New Partner:

I Am Choosing My Happiness Over:

Tatiana's Personal Note: A Simple Reminder That You Have Not Been Forgotten About. God Hears You.

ACT THREE: I AM NOT JUST ANYBODY
MORNING THOUGHTS

Date:					Mood:

Today, I Affirm:			My Future Relationship Will Feel:

I Feel Really Good About:		Today, I Am Asking God:

I Know I Am:				Today I Release _____
					And Hope To Gain:

Today's Relationship With		I Am Excited About:
_____

Looks Like:				Today, I Am Promising Myself:

My New Partner:			I Am Choosing My Happiness Over:

Tatiana's Personal Note: It's Okay To Love Again And Again And Again.

ACT THREE: I AM NOT JUST ANYBODY
MORNING THOUGHTS

Date: Mood:

Today, I Affirm: My Future Relationship Will Feel:

I Feel Really Good About: Today, I Am Asking God:

I Know I Am: Today I Release _____
                                         And Hope To Gain:

Today's Relationship With   I Am Excited About:
_____

Looks Like: Today, I Am Promising Myself:

My New Partner: I Am Choosing My Happiness Over:

*Tatiana's Personal Note: It's Time To Do Some New Things.
Go Somewhere Different And Try Something New.*

ACT THREE: I AM NOT JUST ANYBODY
MORNING THOUGHTS

Date: Mood:

Today, I Affirm: My Future Relationship Will Feel:

I Feel Really Good About: Today, I Am Asking God:

I Know I Am: Today I Release _____
                                         And Hope To Gain:

Today's Relationship With   I Am Excited About:
_____

Looks Like: Today, I Am Promising Myself:

My New Partner: I Am Choosing My Happiness Over:

Tatiana's Personal Note: Someone Is Waiting On You To Notice The Beauty Within Yourself.

I WILL NOT ALLOW SOMEONE TO NEGATIVELY CHANGE MY DEFINITION OF LOVE.

I CAN TREAT HIM
LIKE A KING, BECAUSE
I KNOW HOW TO TREAT
MYSELF LIKE A QUEEN.

ACT THREE: I AM NOT JUST ANYBODY
MORNING THOUGHTS

Date:

Mood:

Today, I Affirm:

My Future Relationship Will Feel:

I Feel Really Good About:

Today, I Am Asking God:

I Know I Am:

Today I Release _____
And Hope To Gain:

Today's Relationship With
_____

I Am Excited About:

Looks Like:

Today, I Am Promising Myself:

My New Partner:

I Am Choosing My Happiness Over:

Tatiana's Personal Note: The Possibilities Of Love Is What Makes Life Amazing. It Can Happen At Anytime.

ACT THREE: I AM NOT JUST ANYBODY
MORNING THOUGHTS

Date: Mood:

Today, I Affirm: My Future Relationship Will Feel:

I Feel Really Good About: Today, I Am Asking God:

I Know I Am: Today I Release _____
                                                And Hope To Gain:

Today's Relationship With   I Am Excited About:
_____

Looks Like: Today, I Am Promising Myself:

My New Partner: I Am Choosing My Happiness Over:

Tatiana's Personal Note: Even When You Do Not Feel Love, Remember That A Lot Of Things That You Have And Are Is Because Of Love.

ACT THREE: I AM NOT JUST ANYBODY
MORNING THOUGHTS

Date:

Today, I Affirm:

I Feel Really Good About:

I Know I Am:

Today's Relationship With

_____

Looks Like:

My New Partner:

Mood:

My Future Relationship Will Feel:

Today, I Am Asking God:

Today I Release _____
And Hope To Gain:

I Am Excited About:

Today, I Am Promising Myself:

I Am Choosing My Happiness Over:

Tatiana's Personal Note: When You're Loved Correctly
You Can Feel It. Stop Fighting For Something You Can't Feel.

ACT THREE: I AM NOT JUST ANYBODY
MORNING THOUGHTS

Date:　　　　　　　　　　　　　　　　Mood:

Today, I Affirm:　　　　　　　　　　　My Future Relationship Will Feel:

I Feel Really Good About:　　　　　　Today, I Am Asking God:

I Know I Am:　　　　　　　　　　　　Today I Release _____
　　　　　　　　　　　　　　　　　　And Hope To Gain:

Today's Relationship With　　　　　　I Am Excited About:
_____

Looks Like:　　　　　　　　　　　　　Today, I Am Promising Myself:

My New Partner:　　　　　　　　　　 I Am Choosing My Happiness Over:

Tatiana's Personal Note: Embrace This Season In Your Life As It Is Preparing You For The Next Amazing Level.

ACT THREE: I AM NOT JUST ANYBODY
MORNING THOUGHTS

Date: Mood:

Today, I Affirm: My Future Relationship Will Feel:

I Feel Really Good About: Today, I Am Asking God:

I Know I Am: Today I Release _____
                                                         And Hope To Gain:

Today's Relationship With   I Am Excited About:
_____

Looks Like: Today, I Am Promising Myself:

My New Partner: I Am Choosing My Happiness Over:

Tatiana's Personal Note: Promise Yourself To Be Present And Enjoy What Many Don't Take The Time To See.

ACT THREE: I AM NOT JUST ANYBODY
MORNING THOUGHTS

Date: Mood:

Today, I Affirm: My Future Relationship Will Feel:

I Feel Really Good About: Today, I Am Asking God:

I Know I Am: Today I Release _____
                                               And Hope To Gain:

Today's Relationship With   I Am Excited About:
_____

Looks Like: Today, I Am Promising Myself:

My New Partner: I Am Choosing My Happiness Over:

Tatiana's Personal Note: Feel The Love That You Want Daily.

ACT THREE: I AM NOT JUST ANYBODY
MORNING THOUGHTS

Date: Mood:

Today, I Affirm: My Future Relationship Will Feel:

I Feel Really Good About: Today, I Am Asking God:

I Know I Am: Today I Release _____
                                               And Hope To Gain:

Today's Relationship With   I Am Excited About:
_____

Looks Like: Today, I Am Promising Myself:

My New Partner: I Am Choosing My Happiness Over:

Tatiana's Personal Note: Notice That The Greatest Moments Of Your Life Were Never Forced.

ACT THREE: I AM NOT JUST ANYBODY
MORNING THOUGHTS

Date:	Mood:

Today, I Affirm:	My Future Relationship Will Feel:

I Feel Really Good About:	Today, I Am Asking God:

I Know I Am:	Today I Release _____
	And Hope To Gain:

Today's Relationship With	I Am Excited About:
_____

Looks Like:	Today, I Am Promising Myself:

My New Partner:	I Am Choosing My Happiness Over:

Tatiana's Personal Note: Your Love Towards Others Is Needed.

THE HEALED ME
FEELS SO GOOD.

ME. THE MOST BEAUTIFUL WOMAN I KNOW.

ACT THREE: I AM NOT JUST ANYBODY
MORNING THOUGHTS

Date:

Mood:

Today, I Affirm:

My Future Relationship Will Feel:

I Feel Really Good About:

Today, I Am Asking God:

I Know I Am:

Today I Release _____
And Hope To Gain:

Today's Relationship With
_____

I Am Excited About:

Looks Like:

Today, I Am Promising Myself:

My New Partner:

I Am Choosing My Happiness Over:

Tatiana's Personal Note: Choose To Let Things Go.

ACT THREE: I AM NOT JUST ANYBODY
MORNING THOUGHTS

Date: Mood:

Today, I Affirm: My Future Relationship Will Feel:

I Feel Really Good About: Today, I Am Asking God:

I Know I Am: Today I Release _____
                                                                 And Hope To Gain:

Today's Relationship With   I Am Excited About:
_____

Looks Like: Today, I Am Promising Myself:

My New Partner: I Am Choosing My Happiness Over:

Tatiana's Personal Note: To Feel Continuous Love, Always Stay Connected To God.

ACT THREE: I AM NOT JUST ANYBODY
MORNING THOUGHTS

Date: Mood:

Today, I Affirm: My Future Relationship Will Feel:

I Feel Really Good About: Today, I Am Asking God:

I Know I Am: Today I Release _____
                                                   And Hope To Gain:

Today's Relationship With   I Am Excited About:
_____

Looks Like: Today, I Am Promising Myself:

My New Partner: I Am Choosing My Happiness Over:

Tatiana's Personal Note: Give Yourself Permission To Be Loved.

ACT THREE: I AM NOT JUST ANYBODY
MORNING THOUGHTS

Date: Mood:

Today, I Affirm: My Future Relationship Will Feel:

I Feel Really Good About: Today, I Am Asking God:

I Know I Am: Today I Release _____
                                                   And Hope To Gain:

Today's Relationship With   I Am Excited About:
_____

Looks Like: Today, I Am Promising Myself:

My New Partner: I Am Choosing My Happiness Over:

Tatiana's Personal Note: You Deserve Effort And Consistency. You Deserve Friendship And Love.

ACT THREE: I AM NOT JUST ANYBODY
MORNING THOUGHTS

Date:

Mood:

Today, I Affirm:

My Future Relationship Will Feel:

I Feel Really Good About:

Today, I Am Asking God:

I Know I Am:

Today I Release _____
And Hope To Gain:

Today's Relationship With
_____

I Am Excited About:

Looks Like:

Today, I Am Promising Myself:

My New Partner:

I Am Choosing My Happiness Over:

Tatiana's Personal Note: Start Believing Love Belongs To You Because Love Is You.

ACT THREE: I AM NOT JUST ANYBODY
MORNING THOUGHTS

Date: Mood:

Today, I Affirm: My Future Relationship Will Feel:

I Feel Really Good About: Today, I Am Asking God:

I Know I Am: Today I Release _____
                                                         And Hope To Gain:

Today's Relationship With   I Am Excited About:
_____

Looks Like: Today, I Am Promising Myself:

My New Partner: I Am Choosing My Happiness Over:

Tatiana's Personal Note: Allow Others To Love You. Every Part Of You.

ACT THREE: I AM NOT JUST ANYBODY
MORNING THOUGHTS

Date:

Mood:

Today, I Affirm:

My Future Relationship Will Feel:

I Feel Really Good About:

Today, I Am Asking God:

I Know I Am:

Today I Release _____ And Hope To Gain:

Today's Relationship With
_____

I Am Excited About:

Looks Like:

Today, I Am Promising Myself:

My New Partner:

I Am Choosing My Happiness Over:

Tatiana's Personal Note: Find Your Peace And Stay There.

HAPPY ME IS SO PRETTY.

I AM GORGEOUS, AND THE STANDARDS ARE VERY, VERY, VERY HIGH.

ACT THREE: I AM NOT JUST ANYBODY
MORNING THOUGHTS

Date:

Mood:

Today, I Affirm:

My Future Relationship Will Feel:

I Feel Really Good About:

Today, I Am Asking God:

I Know I Am:

Today I Release _____
And Hope To Gain:

Today's Relationship With

_____

I Am Excited About:

Looks Like:

Today, I Am Promising Myself:

My New Partner:

I Am Choosing My Happiness Over:

Tatiana's Personal Note: You Can't Hide From Love.

ACT THREE: I AM NOT JUST ANYBODY
MORNING THOUGHTS

Date:

Mood:

Today, I Affirm:

My Future Relationship Will Feel:

I Feel Really Good About:

Today, I Am Asking God:

I Know I Am:

Today I Release _____
And Hope To Gain:

Today's Relationship With
_____

I Am Excited About:

Looks Like:

Today, I Am Promising Myself:

My New Partner:

I Am Choosing My Happiness Over:

Tatiana's Personal Note: You Can See Love Through Actions.

ACT THREE: I AM NOT JUST ANYBODY
MORNING THOUGHTS

Date:

Mood:

Today, I Affirm:

My Future Relationship Will Feel:

I Feel Really Good About:

Today, I Am Asking God:

I Know I Am:

Today I Release _____
And Hope To Gain:

Today's Relationship With
_____

I Am Excited About:

Looks Like:

Today, I Am Promising Myself:

My New Partner:

I Am Choosing My Happiness Over:

Tatiana's Personal Note: Choose To Always Respond With Love.

ACT THREE: I AM NOT JUST ANYBODY
MORNING THOUGHTS

Date: Mood:

Today, I Affirm: My Future Relationship Will Feel:

I Feel Really Good About: Today, I Am Asking God:

I Know I Am: Today I Release _____
                                         And Hope To Gain:

Today's Relationship With   I Am Excited About:
_____

Looks Like: Today, I Am Promising Myself:

My New Partner: I Am Choosing My Happiness Over:

Tatiana's Personal Note: It Feels Good To Be In The Process Of Healing.

ACT THREE: I AM NOT JUST ANYBODY
MORNING THOUGHTS

Date: Mood:

Today, I Affirm: My Future Relationship Will Feel:

I Feel Really Good About: Today, I Am Asking God:

I Know I Am: Today I Release _____
                                                   And Hope To Gain:

Today's Relationship With   I Am Excited About:
_____

Looks Like: Today, I Am Promising Myself:

My New Partner: I Am Choosing My Happiness Over:

Tatiana's Personal Note: Choose To No Longer Lose Yourself When Learning To Love Someone Else.

ACT THREE: I AM NOT JUST ANYBODY
MORNING THOUGHTS

Date:

Mood:

Today, I Affirm:

My Future Relationship Will Feel:

I Feel Really Good About:

Today, I Am Asking God:

I Know I Am:

Today I Release _____
And Hope To Gain:

Today's Relationship With
_____

I Am Excited About:

Looks Like:

Today, I Am Promising Myself:

My New Partner:

I Am Choosing My Happiness Over:

Tatiana's Personal Note: Use Your Words To Create Your New Life.

ACT THREE: I AM NOT JUST ANYBODY
MORNING THOUGHTS

Date: Mood:

Today, I Affirm: My Future Relationship Will Feel:

I Feel Really Good About: Today, I Am Asking God:

I Know I Am: Today I Release _____
                                                    And Hope To Gain:

Today's Relationship With   I Am Excited About:
_____

Looks Like: Today, I Am Promising Myself:

My New Partner: I Am Choosing My Happiness Over:

Tatiana's Personal Note: How You Choose To Love Yourself Is Important.

ACT THREE: I AM NOT JUST ANYBODY
MORNING THOUGHTS

Date: Mood:

Today, I Affirm: My Future Relationship Will Feel:

I Feel Really Good About: Today, I Am Asking God:

I Know I Am: Today I Release _____
                                                And Hope To Gain:

Today's Relationship With   I Am Excited About:
_____

Looks Like: Today, I Am Promising Myself:

My New Partner: I Am Choosing My Happiness Over:

Tatiana's Personal Note: Your Prayers Get Attention.

THERE IS MORE THAN
ENOUGH LOVE TO LAST A
MILLION LIFETIMES.
- I PROMISE

I JUST KEEP GETTING BETTER.

ACT THREE: I AM NOT JUST ANYBODY
MORNING THOUGHTS

Date:

Mood:

Today, I Affirm:

My Future Relationship Will Feel:

I Feel Really Good About:

Today, I Am Asking God:

I Know I Am:

Today I Release _____ And Hope To Gain:

Today's Relationship With
_____

I Am Excited About:

Looks Like:

Today, I Am Promising Myself:

My New Partner:

I Am Choosing My Happiness Over:

Tatiana's Personal Note: Others Will See You The Way You See Yourself.

ACT THREE: I AM NOT JUST ANYBODY
MORNING THOUGHTS

Date: Mood:

Today, I Affirm: My Future Relationship Will Feel:

I Feel Really Good About: Today, I Am Asking God:

I Know I Am: Today I Release _____
                                                         And Hope To Gain:

Today's Relationship With   I Am Excited About:
_____

Looks Like: Today, I Am Promising Myself:

My New Partner: I Am Choosing My Happiness Over:

Tatiana's Personal Note: Love Yourself And Know Your Worth.

ACT THREE: I AM NOT JUST ANYBODY
MORNING THOUGHTS

Date: Mood:

Today, I Affirm: My Future Relationship Will Feel:

I Feel Really Good About: Today, I Am Asking God:

I Know I Am: Today I Release _____
                                         And Hope To Gain:

Today's Relationship With   I Am Excited About:
_____

Looks Like: Today, I Am Promising Myself:

My New Partner: I Am Choosing My Happiness Over:

Tatiana's Personal Note: Stay Faithful In Believing In New Love.

ACT THREE: I AM NOT JUST ANYBODY
MORNING THOUGHTS

Date:

Mood:

Today, I Affirm:

My Future Relationship Will Feel:

I Feel Really Good About:

Today, I Am Asking God:

I Know I Am:

Today I Release _____
And Hope To Gain:

Today's Relationship With
_____

I Am Excited About:

Looks Like:

Today, I Am Promising Myself:

My New Partner:

I Am Choosing My Happiness Over:

Tatiana's Personal Note: True And Unconditional Love Replenishes And Forgives.

ACT THREE: I AM NOT JUST ANYBODY
MORNING THOUGHTS

Date: Mood:

Today, I Affirm: My Future Relationship Will Feel:

I Feel Really Good About: Today, I Am Asking God:

I Know I Am: Today I Release _____
And Hope To Gain:

Today's Relationship With I Am Excited About:
_____

Looks Like: Today, I Am Promising Myself:

My New Partner: I Am Choosing My Happiness Over:

Tatiana's Personal Note: Do Not Allow Anything To Stop You From Being You.

ACT THREE: I AM NOT JUST ANYBODY
MORNING THOUGHTS

Date: Mood:

Today, I Affirm: My Future Relationship Will Feel:

I Feel Really Good About: Today, I Am Asking God:

I Know I Am: Today I Release _____
                                                  And Hope To Gain:

Today's Relationship With   I Am Excited About:
_____

Looks Like: Today, I Am Promising Myself:

My New Partner: I Am Choosing My Happiness Over:

Tatiana's Personal Note: Protect Your Space. Protect Your Peace.

ACT THREE: I AM NOT JUST ANYBODY
MORNING THOUGHTS

Date: Mood:

Today, I Affirm: My Future Relationship Will Feel:

I Feel Really Good About: Today, I Am Asking God:

I Know I Am: Today I Release _____
                                                    And Hope To Gain:

Today's Relationship With   I Am Excited About:
_____

Looks Like: Today, I Am Promising Myself:

My New Partner: I Am Choosing My Happiness Over:

Tatiana's Personal Note: Be The Source To Your Happiness.

ACT THREE: I AM NOT JUST ANYBODY
MORNING THOUGHTS

Date:

Mood:

Today, I Affirm:

My Future Relationship Will Feel:

I Feel Really Good About:

Today, I Am Asking God:

I Know I Am:

Today I Release _____
And Hope To Gain:

Today's Relationship With

_____

I Am Excited About:

Looks Like:

Today, I Am Promising Myself:

My New Partner:

I Am Choosing My Happiness Over:

Tatiana's Personal Note: May Your Happiness Be Unconditional.

I HAVE ACCEPTED MYSELF AND SOON THE RIGHT PERSON WILL MORE THAN ACCEPT ME TOO.

LOVE IS PATIENT, LOVE IS KIND. IT DOES NOT ENVY, IT DOES NOT BOAST, IT IS NOT PROUD. IT DOES NOT DISHONOR OTHERS, IT IS NOT SELF-SEEKING, IT IS NOT EASILY ANGERED, IT KEEPS NO RECORD OF WRONGS. LOVE DOES NOT DELIGHT IN EVIL BUT REJOICES WITH THE TRUTH. IT ALWAYS PROTECTS, ALWAYS TRUSTS, ALWAYS HOPES, ALWAYS PERSEVERES.
- 1 CORINTHIANS 13:4-7

ACT THREE: I AM NOT JUST ANYBODY
MORNING THOUGHTS

Date: Mood:

Today, I Affirm: My Future Relationship Will Feel:

I Feel Really Good About: Today, I Am Asking God:

I Know I Am: Today I Release _____
                                                   And Hope To Gain:

Today's Relationship With   I Am Excited About:
_____

Looks Like: Today, I Am Promising Myself:

My New Partner: I Am Choosing My Happiness Over:

Tatiana's Personal Note: Show The World How Amazing You Are.

ACT THREE: I AM NOT JUST ANYBODY
MORNING THOUGHTS

Date:	Mood:

Today, I Affirm:	My Future Relationship Will Feel:

I Feel Really Good About:	Today, I Am Asking God:

I Know I Am:	Today I Release _____
 And Hope To Gain:

Today's Relationship With	I Am Excited About:
_____

Looks Like:	Today, I Am Promising Myself:

My New Partner:	I Am Choosing My Happiness Over:

Tatiana's Personal Note: You Are Filled With Favor. Others See It, So Should You.

ACT THREE: I AM NOT JUST ANYBODY
MORNING THOUGHTS

Date: Mood:

Today, I Affirm: My Future Relationship Will Feel:

I Feel Really Good About: Today, I Am Asking God:

I Know I Am: Today I Release _____
                                                               And Hope To Gain:

Today's Relationship With   I Am Excited About:
_____

Looks Like: Today, I Am Promising Myself:

My New Partner: I Am Choosing My Happiness Over:

Tatiana's Personal Note: Get Ready For Your Love Breakthrough.

ACT THREE: I AM NOT JUST ANYBODY
MORNING THOUGHTS

Date: Mood:

Today, I Affirm: My Future Relationship Will Feel:

I Feel Really Good About: Today, I Am Asking God:

I Know I Am: Today I Release _____
                                                       And Hope To Gain:

Today's Relationship With   I Am Excited About:
_____

Looks Like: Today, I Am Promising Myself:

My New Partner: I Am Choosing My Happiness Over:

Tatiana's Personal Note: Command Full Undivided Attention By Simply Being You.

ACT THREE: I AM NOT JUST ANYBODY
MORNING THOUGHTS

Date: Mood:

Today, I Affirm: My Future Relationship Will Feel:

I Feel Really Good About: Today, I Am Asking God:

I Know I Am: Today I Release _____
                                                And Hope To Gain:

Today's Relationship With
_____   I Am Excited About:

Looks Like: Today, I Am Promising Myself:

My New Partner: I Am Choosing My Happiness Over:

==Tatiana's Personal Note: You Are As Amazing As You Say You Are.==

ACT THREE: I AM NOT JUST ANYBODY
MORNING THOUGHTS

Date: Mood:

Today, I Affirm: My Future Relationship Will Feel:

I Feel Really Good About: Today, I Am Asking God:

I Know I Am: Today I Release _____
                                                   And Hope To Gain:

Today's Relationship With   I Am Excited About:
_____

Looks Like: Today, I Am Promising Myself:

My New Partner: I Am Choosing My Happiness Over:

Tatiana's Personal Note: Things Are Changing For The Better.

ACT THREE: I AM NOT JUST ANYBODY

MORNING THOUGHTS

Date: Mood:

Today, I Affirm: My Future Relationship Will Feel:

I Feel Really Good About: Today, I Am Asking God:

I Know I Am: Today I Release _____
                                                   And Hope To Gain:

Today's Relationship With   I Am Excited About:
_____

Looks Like: Today, I Am Promising Myself:

My New Partner: I Am Choosing My Happiness Over:

Tatiana's Personal Note: Don't Ever Worry About How Bright Your Light Is.

ACT THREE: I AM NOT JUST ANYBODY
MORNING THOUGHTS

Date: Mood:

Today, I Affirm: My Future Relationship Will Feel:

I Feel Really Good About: Today, I Am Asking God:

I Know I Am: Today I Release _____
                                                          And Hope To Gain:

Today's Relationship With   I Am Excited About:
_____

Looks Like: Today, I Am Promising Myself:

My New Partner: I Am Choosing My Happiness Over:

Tatiana's Personal Note: Always Believe Love Will Make Its Way To You.

ACT THREE: I AM NOT JUST ANYBODY
MORNING THOUGHTS

Date:

Today, I Affirm:

I Feel Really Good About:

I Know I Am:

Today's Relationship With
_____

Looks Like:

My New Partner:

Mood:

My Future Relationship Will Feel:

Today, I Am Asking God:

Today I Release _____
And Hope To Gain:

I Am Excited About:

Today, I Am Promising Myself:

I Am Choosing My Happiness Over:

Tatiana's Personal Note: Don't Ever Under-Estimate The Power Of Your Love.

ACT THREE: I AM NOT JUST ANYBODY
MORNING THOUGHTS

Date:

Mood:

Today, I Affirm:

My Future Relationship Will Feel:

I Feel Really Good About:

Today, I Am Asking God:

I Know I Am:

Today I Release _____
And Hope To Gain:

Today's Relationship With
_____

I Am Excited About:

Looks Like:

Today, I Am Promising Myself:

My New Partner:

I Am Choosing My Happiness Over:

Tatiana's Personal Note: It's Okay To Fall In Love .... All Over Again.

AND THEN
GOD BLESSED ME....

BECAUSE OF GOD,
I AM LOVED ALWAYS.
IN ALL WAYS.

RECLAIM YOURSELF
AFFIRMATION CARDS

HOW TO USE YOUR RECLAIM YOURSELF AFFIRMATION CARDS

We are delighted to present an exquisite collection of 100 affirmation cards, meticulously curated to guide you through the delicate process of healing after a breakup. These affirmations are thoughtfully designed to help you navigate the emotional intricacies of heartache, while gently nurturing a renewed sense of self-worth and profound self-love. Begin by carefully separating each affirmation card from the gilded pages. These elegantly crafted cards will serve as daily reminders of your inherent value, offering solace and strength as you embark on your personal journey of recovery.

To fully immerse yourself in the transformative power of these affirmations, integrate them into your daily routine with intention. Select a few cards each day and reflect deeply on their messages, either by softly reciting them aloud or meditating on them in quiet contemplation. This ritual of positive reinforcement will gradually fortify your self-esteem, cultivating a tender and compassionate relationship with yourself. Through consistent engagement, you will reaffirm a narrative of self-worth, emotional resilience, and renewed confidence as you embrace your healing journey.

It is essential to remain steadfast in this practice, even during moments when motivation wanes or when the affirmations feel less effective. The repetition of these empowering statements, regardless of temporary resistance or doubt, plays a vital role in reshaping your mindset. By committing to this daily ritual, you will foster a deeper, enduring love for yourself, ultimately restoring your readiness to embrace future relationships with grace, confidence, and unwavering self-assurance.

LET'S GET STARTED

RECLAIM YOURSELF AFFIRMATION CARDS

I Believe In My Resilience And Strength. TAIYE	I Believe I Am Worthy Of Love. TAIYE
I Believe I Can Overcome This Heartbreak. TAIYE	I Believe In My Ability To Heal. TAIYE
I Believe I Am Capable Of Finding Happiness Again. TAIYE	I Believe I Am A Worthy And Deserving Individual. TAIYE
I Believe I Am Loved And Supported. TAIYE	I Believe In The Power Of Self-Love. TAIYE
I Believe I Can Create A Beautiful Life For Myself. TAIYE	I Believe In The Future Of My Love Life. TAIYE

RECLAIM YOURSELF AFFIRMATION CARDS

I Feel Like A Star, With A Self-Worth That Shines As Bright As My Smile.

TAIYE

I Feel Grateful For The Lessons That Have Made Me Even More Fabulous.

TAIYE

I Feel Empowered To Create My Own Happiness And Sparkle With Joy.

TAIYE

I Feel Confident In Attracting Relationships That Match My Dazzling Spirit.

TAIYE

I Feel Excited About The Fabulous Adventures That Lie Ahead.

TAIYE

I Feel A Deep Love For The Unique And Extraordinary Person I Am.

TAIYE

I Feel Comforted By The Love And Care I Lavish Upon Myself.

TAIYE

I Feel Confident In Creating A Joyful And Radiant Life.

TAIYE

I Feel Proud Of The Person I'm Becoming Through My Own Self-Love.

TAIYE

I Feel A Deep Connection To My Inner Strength And Resilience.

TAIYE

RECLAIM YOURSELF AFFIRMATION CARDS

I Feel Excited About The Endless Possibilities The Future Holds. TAIYE	I Feel A Profound Peace, Beautiful, As I Embrace My Own Worth And Beauty. TAIYE
I Feel Grateful For The Support And Love That Surrounds Me. TAIYE	I Feel Confident In My Ability To Attract And Nurture Loving Relationships. TAIYE
I Feel Proud Of The Strength And Courage I Discover In Myself. TAIYE	I Feel Joyful In The Company Of My Own Fabulous Self. TAIYE
I Feel Serene As I Embrace And Celebrate My Own Uniqueness. TAIYE	I Feel At Peace With The Person I Am Becoming. TAIYE
I Feel Excited For The Positive Changes And New Experiences Coming My Way. TAIYE	I Feel A Deep Love For The Person I Am And The Journey I'm On. TAIYE

RECLAIM YOURSELF AFFIRMATION CARDS

I Feel A Beautiful Sense Of Hope For The Future That Is Unfolding. TAIYE	I Feel Confident In My Ability To Find And Create Happiness. TAIYE
I Feel A Profound Sense Of Accomplishment From My Journey Of Healing. TAIYE	I Feel Empowered To Trust And Believe In My Own Worth. TAIYE
I Feel A Deep Sense Of Self-Acceptance That Shines From Within. TAIYE	I Feel A Glamorous Sense Of Adventure In The Possibilities Of My Life. TAIYE
I Feel Grateful For The Love And Support I Have From Within And Around Me. TAIYE	I Love Myself Just As Much As Any Star Loves The Spotlight. TAIYE
I Love The Person I'm Becoming Through This Journey Of Healing. TAIYE	I Love The Positive Changes Unfolding In My Life, Making Me Even More Fabulous. TAIYE

RECLAIM YOURSELF AFFIRMATION CARDS

I Love The Self-Compassion I Shower On Myself. TAIYE	I Love The Confidence And Grace I Embody Every Single Day. TAIYE
I Love The New Beginnings In My Life. TAIYE	I Love The Strength And Wisdom I Gain. TAIYE
I Love The Person I'm Becoming As I Embrace My True Self. TAIYE	I Love The Way I'm Learning To Celebrate My Own Unique Charm. TAIYE
I Love The Deep Inner Strength I Possess. TAIYE	I Love The Positive Energy I Attract. TAIYE
I Love The Way I'm Learning To Trust And Believe In Myself. TAIYE	I Love The Compassion And Understanding I Offer Myself, Beautiful And Gentle. TAIYE

RECLAIM YOURSELF AFFIRMATION CARDS

I Love The Deep Sense Of Self-Worth I'm Building. TAIYE	I Believe In My Ability To Heal And Find Happiness Again. TAIYE
I Believe That My Heart Is Resilient And Strong. TAIYE	I Believe In The Value Of My Own Self-Love And Self-Care. TAIYE
I Believe That I Am Worthy Of A Love That Respects And Cherishes Me. TAIYE	I Believe That My Past Does Not Define My Future. TAIYE
I Believe That Each Day Brings New Opportunities For Growth And Joy. TAIYE	I Believe In My Capacity To Find Peace And Contentment Within Myself. TAIYE
I Believe That I Deserve A Relationship That Nurtures And Supports Me. TAIYE	I Believe That Healing Is A Journey That I Am Fully Equipped To Undertake. TAIYE

RECLAIM YOURSELF AFFIRMATION CARDS

I Believe That I Am Deserving Of Love And Happiness Simply Because I Exist. TAIYE	I Believe In The Power Of Letting Go To Make Space For New Beginnings. TAIYE
I Believe That My Heart Will Open Again To Love When I Am Ready. TAIYE	I Believe That I Am Enough Just As I Am. TAIYE
I Believe That Every Experience Teaches Me Something Valuable About Myself. TAIYE	I Believe In My Strength To Overcome Any Challenge. TAIYE
I Believe That My Happiness Is Within My Control. TAIYE	I Believe In The Possibility Of Finding Joy And Fulfillment In My Life. TAIYE
I Believe That My Worth Is Not Determined By Anyone Else's Actions Or Opinions. TAIYE	I Believe That Healing Comes From Within And I Am Taking Steps Toward It Every Day. TAIYE

RECLAIM YOURSELF AFFIRMATION CARDS

I Believe In The Beauty Of My Journey And The Lessons It Brings. TAIYE	I Believe That I Am Attracting Positive And Loving Experiences Into My Life. TAIYE
I Believe In My Capacity To Love Myself Fully And Unconditionally. TAIYE	I Believe That Every Ending Is A Chance For A New Beginning. TAIYE
I Believe In My Ability To Rebuild My Life And Create A Future Filled With Joy. TAIYE	I Believe That I Am A Deserving And Lovable Person. TAIYE
I Believe In The Power Of My Own Forgiveness And Healing. TAIYE	I Believe That Love And Happiness Are My Birthright. TAIYE
I Believe That I Am Worthy Of The Deepest, Most Fulfilling Love. TAIYE	I Believe In The Strength Of My Spirit And My Ability To Thrive. TAIYE

RECLAIM YOURSELF AFFIRMATION CARDS

I Believe That My Value Is Intrinsic And Not Dependent On External Validation. TAIYE	I Believe In The Positive Changes That Are Unfolding In My Life. TAIYE
I Believe That I Have The Power To Create The Life I Desire. TAIYE	I Believe In My Own Inner Strength And Resilience. TAIYE
I Believe That I Am Deserving Of All The Love And Joy Life Has To Offer. TAIYE	I Believe That My Heart Is Healing And Becoming Stronger. TAIYE
I Believe In The Importance Of Self-Compassion And Self-Acceptance. TAIYE	I Believe That I Can Find Happiness Within Myself, Regardless Of External Circumstances. TAIYE
I Believe That I Am Worthy Of A Love That Is Kind And Gentle. TAIYE	I Believe That My Future Holds Great Possibilities And New Opportunities For Love. TAIYE

RECLAIM YOURSELF AFFIRMATION CARDS

I Am Beautiful.

TAIYE

I Am Enough.

TAIYE

I Am Valuable.

TAIYE

I Am Lovable.

TAIYE

I Am Everything I Believe I Am.

TAIYE

I Am Sexy.

TAIYE

I Am Love.

TAIYE

I Am Open To Love Again.

TAIYE

I Deserve Happiness.

TAIYE

I Deserve To Be Loved.

TAIYE

Made in the USA
Coppell, TX
13 February 2026